I0393602

U.S. Department of Justice
Office of Justice Programs
810 Seventh Street NW.
Washington, DC 20531

John Ashcroft
Attorney General

Deborah J. Daniels
Assistant Attorney General

Richard R. Nedelkoff
Director, Bureau of Justice Assistance

Office of Justice Programs
World Wide Web Home Page
www.ojp.usdoj.gov

Bureau of Justice Assistance
World Wide Web Home Page
www.ojp.usdoj.gov/BJA

For grant and funding information, contact
U.S. Department of Justice Response Center
1–800–421–6770

NCJ 192278

This document was prepared by Public Technology, Inc., under grant number 1999–DD–BX–K007, awarded by the Bureau of Justice Assistance, Office of Justice Programs, U.S. Department of Justice. The opinions, findings, and conclusions or recommendations expressed in this document are those of the authors and do not necessarily represent the official position or policies of the U.S. Department of Justice.

The Bureau of Justice Assistance is a component of the Office of Justice Programs, which also includes the Bureau of Justice Statistics, the National Institute of Justice, the Office of Juvenile Justice and Delinquency Prevention, and the Office for Victims of Crime.

BJA
Bureau of Justice Assistance

MISSION POSSIBLE

Strong Governance Structures for the
Integration of Justice Information Systems

February 2002   Monograph   NCJ 192278

Mission Possible:
Strong Governance Structures
for the Integration of
Justice Information Systems

Table of Contents

Mission Possible:
Strong Governance Structures
for the Integration of
Justice Information Systems

Figures

Tables

Executive Summary

Public confidence in the United States justice system is negatively impacted by the absence of an integrated justice information system that can share information and provide information that is not only timely, but also accurate and complete. Some jurisdictions have begun planning, and others are implementing, systems that integrate data from several justice agencies within a jurisdiction and among jurisdictions within a region or state. To enhance the efforts of local jurisdictions engaged in justice information systems integration and to encourage similar efforts in other jurisdictions, Public Technology, Inc. (PTI) conducted a study that examined justice integration governance structures at the local government level. The study builds upon the recommendations from a series of U.S. Department of Justice-sponsored conferences that focused on local and state information system integration. Through PTI's study, information from the field was compiled and analyzed to ascertain the type, quality, and capability of existing justice information integration and governance structure models.

Surveys were completed by 251 jurisdictional representatives of suburban, urban, and rural areas throughout the United States. The majority of respondents were engaged in some aspect of information systems integration with other departments and/or agencies, and most systems were integrated with their state justice system. However, one-third had no integration efforts underway and no governance structure in place to facilitate integration.

Some of the major findings of the study were:

- Funding is a major reason that jurisdictions are not engaged in justice information system integration and that they have not established governance structures.

- Other obstacles are turf issues and lack of technology.

- Local jurisdictions believe that the federal and state governments can best assist them by providing funding for their integration efforts. Regional governments could help best by providing strategic planning and funding assistance; and local governments could best assist by providing the appropriate personnel and implementation support.

- The most common type of governance structure was established through a cooperative agreement.

- Governance structures are most often initiated by persons directly affected by the structure and/or by key advocates.

- The roles and responsibilities of a governance board vary, but the most common include reviewing projects and prioritizing initiatives.

- Law enforcement is most commonly the agency involved in integration efforts. The top three information systems that respondents integrated were records management, offender history, and computer dispatch systems.

- The majority of respondents felt having a governance structure was a benefit to integration.

- In jurisdictions that have not established a governance structure, integration tends to be managed by an individual agency.

Based on their experiences with justice information system integration, respondents offered a number of suggestions for advancing these efforts. In establishing local governance structures that can facilitate the integration of justice information systems, several central themes emerged from the recommendations:

- Ensure equal involvement/participation from all agencies/ jurisdictions involved.
- Explore and secure funding.
- Set realistic goals and objectives with a reasonable implementation timeframe.
- Keep ongoing, open lines of communication with all agencies/jurisdictions involved.
- Have unconditional support of county boards/ city councils/elected officials.
- Have well-trained technology users.
- Standardize and network all software, hardware, and protocols.

Well-defined governance structures improve the justice information integration process by enhancing communication, establishing guidelines and policies, reducing turf battles, and fostering coordination and cooperation. Such structures consolidate and streamline information integration. Governance structures also can play a crucial role in securing funding for local system integration efforts. Technology, by itself, cannot solve all system integration problems, and even the best-equipped integration effort will soon bog down without an effective governing body to chart its course.

The PTI study shows that all governance structures do not have to be created in the same way. Jurisdictions/agencies or clusters of agencies have to decide what works best for them and design their structures accordingly. Nevertheless, each structure should have, at a minimum, a document that sets forth its goals and objectives, establishes the decision-making process, and identifies the committee participants and their responsibilities.

Survey respondents identified leadership as critical to the success of justice information integration. Structures must be established in such a way that they will not be negatively affected by periodic changes in locally elected and appointed leadership. Each governance structure needs a committed champion who will work to ensure smooth working relationships and who will keep the integration efforts moving forward.

Acknowledgments

Public Technology, Inc. (PTI) is the Washington, D.C.-based nonprofit technology research, development, and commercialization organization of the National League of Cities, the National Association of Counties, and the International City/County Management Association. PTI's mission is to bring the benefits of technology to local government.

Participants in the Governance Project are

Vance Arnett, Director of Community Programs, Office of the State Attorney for the Sixth Judicial Circuit of Florida, Clearwater, Florida; Douglas Bartosh, Chief of Police, Scottsdale, Arizona; Patrice Bataglia, County Commissioner, Dakota County, Minnesota; Chris Bosch, Chief Fire Marshall, Kansas City Fire Department, Kansas City, Missouri; Rich Cinfio, Commander, San Carlos Police Department, San Carlos, California; Connie Dillard, Technology Manager, San Carlos, California; Mike Dunbaugh, Chief of Police, Santa Rosa, California; Jerry Farris, Information Technology Director, Winston-Salem, North Carolina; Gerald E. Hardt, Program Manager, Criminal Justice Records, Arizona Criminal Justice Commission, Phoenix, Arizona; Ron Hass, Criminal Justice Senior Technology Manager, Department of Telecommunications and Information Services, San Francisco, California; Clint Hubbard, Information Systems Officer, Albuquerque, New Mexico; Randy Johnson, County Commissioner, Hennepin County, Minnesota; Debbie Kerschner, Community Corrections, Dakota County, Minnesota; Winifred Lyday, Policy Advisor, Office of Justice Programs, U.S. Department of Justice, Washington, DC; Bill Mills, City Attorney's Office, Criminal Division, Tucson, Arizona; Ron Olin, Chief of Police, Lawrence, Kansas; Jim Peschong, Assistant Chief of Police, Lincoln, Nebraska; Major Kathleen Pierce, Commander, Information Systems Division, Kansas City Police Department, Kansas City, Missouri; Tom Russell, Regional Computer Center, Cincinnati, Ohio; C.J. Shaffer, Director, Plans, Analysis and Emergency Operations Branch, Hampton Police Department, Hampton, Virginia; and Barbara Sheen Todd, County Commissioner, Pinellas County, Florida.

Site visit team members are

Norm Bowman, Citywide GIS Coordinator, Kansas City, Missouri; Will Davis, Police Planning Manager, Scottsdale Police Department, Scottsdale, Arizona; Mike Nagan, Director, Information Services, Seattle, Washington; Pam Scanlon, ARJIS Regional Director, San Diego Police Department, San Diego, California; and Ron Wilborg, Grants and Contracts Supervisor, Community Corrections, Hennepin County, Minnesota.

Janet Quist, former Director of Public Safety Programs at PTI, and writer Elsie Scott, Senior Executive, Office of Chief of Police, Washington, D.C., contributed to this project.

Chapter 1
Introduction: The Local Governance Survey

Purpose

Through a cooperative agreement with the U.S. Department of Justice's Office of Justice Programs (OJP), Public Technology, Inc. (PTI) examined the types of structures that local governments either use or are contemplating to implement or oversee justice information systems integration efforts.

PTI is the only nonprofit technology organization for local governments in the United States whose mission is to advance the development and use of technology by local government. The National League of Cities, the National Association of Counties, and the International City/County Management Association, three leading national and international organizations representing city and county government, provide PTI with its policy direction, while a select group of city and county members conduct applied research and development and technology transfer functions. Created in 1971, PTI is the only national organization dedicated to furthering the use of technology in both cities and counties, for both elected officials and professional managers. Partnerships with private industry, an entrepreneurial spirit, and a focus on connectivity, sustainability, and wise decision support are the foundations of PTI's philosophy.

For this project, PTI conducted a mail survey with followup site visits to six local jurisdictions selected based on their survey responses, population size, geographic diversity, and levels of their integration governance efforts. The purpose of this study was to

- Ascertain the type, quality, and capability of governance processes and structures in use or contemplated nationwide.
- Evaluate the quality and effectiveness of current models.
- Explore the creative processes behind various governance structures.
- Observe the progress of different communities as they seek to share justice information.

By achieving total integration, PTI believes that local governments will be better positioned to respond to the increasing public pressure for faster, more effective justice services.

Methodology

The first task of this project was to survey local governments to examine governance structures facilitating the integration of justice information systems at the local level. A group of 23 city and county public safety professionals and local elected officials representing PTI's membership was convened for the task of drafting the survey and later, once results were in, drafting the content of the guidebook. Working group members represented a broad range of experts with direct experience in the area of local justice information systems and the technologies and governance structures needed to successfully integrate these systems. Participants included professionals representing city and county law enforcement, courts, current managers of integrated justice information systems, public safety and jurisdictionwide information technology professionals, emergency operations professionals, criminal records managers, fire personnel, and elected county officials. One state-level representative also participated.

The group used the "Collaboratory," a completely portable, customized electronic workspace consisting of laptop computers and collaborative decision-support software. Using professional, experienced facilitators and technical support, this tool promotes open discussion and brainstorming using a network of personal computers through which participants simultaneously and anonymously submit ideas and reach consensus on difficult issues.

Once the draft survey was completed, PTI worked with The Leede Research Group from Manitowoc, Wisconsin, to formalize and administer the survey. PTI worked with its three sponsoring organizations to obtain a sampling of each organization's membership. Approximately 250 cities and counties were chosen from their respective databases using population size and geography as selection criteria (see appendix B: Jurisdictions Responding to Survey).

Because the diversity of agencies and individuals involved in justice systems at the local level varies among jurisdictions, the survey was sent to the chief elected or appointed official of each jurisdiction. The recipient was then asked to forward it to appropriate individual(s) within the respective agencies for a response. As is noted in the data, the law enforcement agency was the most likely to respond. It should be noted that there were issues regarding those jurisdictions with more than one agency involved in integration, since only one agency was likely to complete the form. This respondent might not be fully aware of what the other agencies were doing, resulting in a response that may have been based solely on that respondent's particular perspective.

More than 1,300 surveys were sent out. With the exception of PTI's membership, the surveys were directed to the chief local elected or appointed official. Most responses were provided by persons with immediate knowledge concerning local integration (i.e., mainly justice professionals). Respondents could return the survey by mail, fax, or online via PTI's Web site.

The survey instrument consisted of 64 open- and closed-ended multiple choice questions (see Appendix A). With the exception of a few demographic questions designed to enable comparisons among jurisdictions, questions were designed to elicit information concerning the status of justice integration efforts and governance structures at the local government level. PTI examined the way governance structures were created (e.g., whether by statute, arising from a series of informal meetings among staff wanting to improve efficiency or improve current processes, etc.), the reasons that some succeeded and some failed, and the types of resources necessary to create and sustain effective governance structures. A working group comprising representatives from a broad range of city and county justice agencies and elected officials collaborated to draft the survey and the contents of this guidebook.

The responses were tallied and the data analyzed during March 2000. Surveys were completed and returned by 251 respondents, constituting an 18.5% response rate. The error rate associated with the survey was +/- 5.59% at a 95% confidence level.

Survey Respondents

Jurisdictions located in suburban and urban areas made up 68% of the responses, while rural jurisdictions accounted for 19%; 13% of the respondents (DK/NA) did not indicate a geographic location (see figure 1).

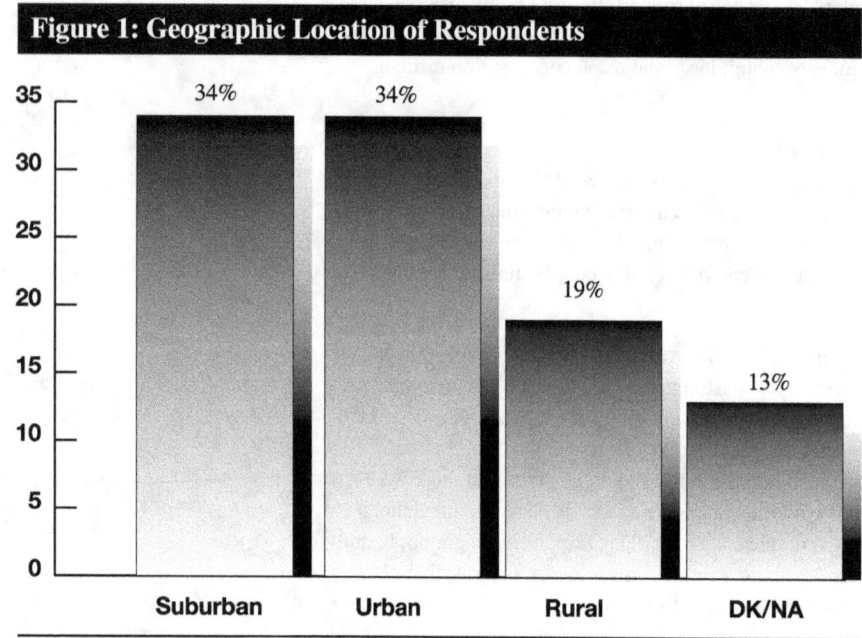

Figure 1: Geographic Location of Respondents

Over one-third of the responding jurisdictions (38%) were located in communities with populations of between 10,000 and 50,000 people, and one-fifth (20%) were located in areas with populations of more than 250,000 people (see figure 2). *Note: The percentages do not total to 100% because some respondents did not answer the question.*

The largest group of responding jurisdictions was cities (63%); the second largest group, 22%, was counties (see figure 3). The most common form of government was council-manager (39%), with 29% having a mayor-council form of government (see figure 3).

The majority of the responding jurisdictions reported that their jurisdiction operates information systems that are integrated with other departments/agencies. Two common factors were found. First, most jurisdictions were integrated with their respective state's justice

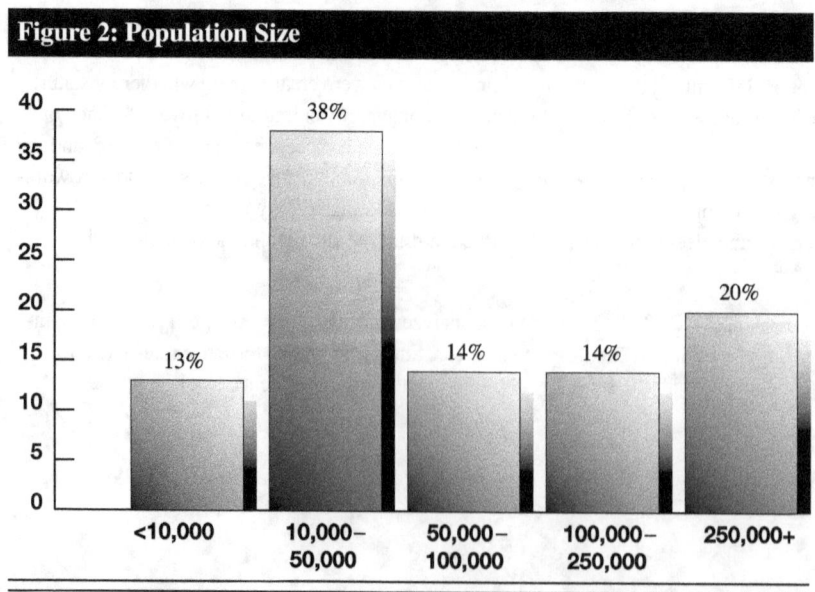

Figure 2: Population Size

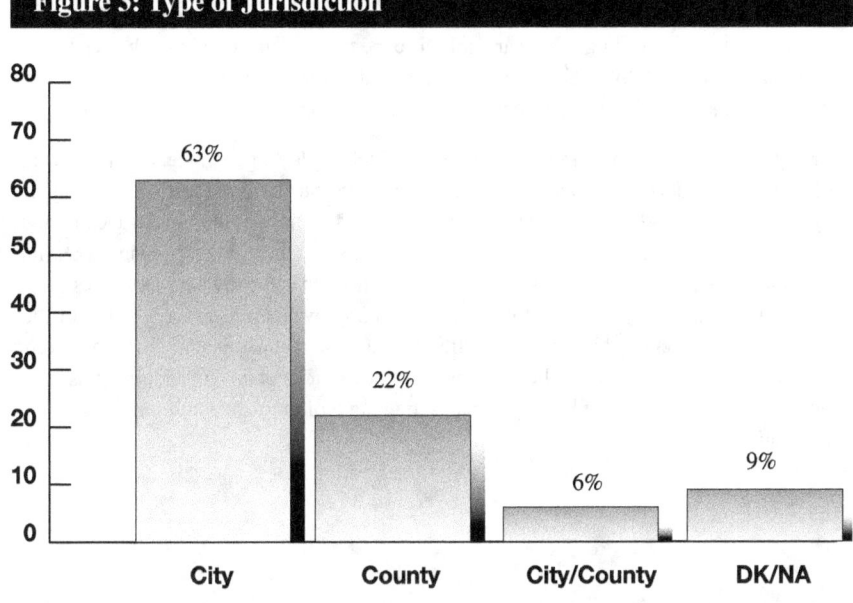

Figure 3: Type of Jurisdiction

information system and, second, most had not yet developed an integrated information technology strategic plan.

Analyzing this data, PTI found that most jurisdictions involved in some phase of justice system integration have

- Identified a governing body, the composition of which is suited to their environment.
- Devised a governance structure that guides that body's operation.
- Set policies that increased their chances for success.
- Created an environment of trust.

To provide a clear blueprint for successful integration of justice information systems, a site visit team visited six jurisdictions representing a broad spectrum of local governments. Site visits were selected based on survey responses, population size, geographic diversity, and levels of integration/governance effort. Those visits proved invaluable for both supporting empirical survey data and understanding the application of current governance structures.

Purpose of Guidebook

This guidebook is designed to help jurisdictions create and deploy governance for the integration of their justice information systems. Survey data, coupled with case studies, combine for a compelling study of how to accomplish better information integration through governance. This guidebook helps provide the tools local governments need to develop successful governance structures and improve upon existing structures. It can enhance the capability and capacity of local governments to move toward the horizontal and vertical integration of justice information sharing systems.

The impetus for developing this guidebook did not come from a Federal Government mandate. It came from the grassroots—from the potential users at the local government level. The OJP conference series discussed in the next chapter made obvious the need to support existing integration efforts and to provide agencies not currently engaged in integration with assistance in getting started. Before the mechanisms providing the needed assistance could be fully established, however, a status assessment needed to be conducted. The PTI survey was the vehicle used to accomplish this.

This guidebook is an initial step in the process of helping local governments reach a level of integration that could lead to a nationwide, seamless integration of justice information systems. Local jurisdictions that do not have structures in place or are not engaged in justice information integration can use the guidebook to assist them in developing successful data integration and governance structures. Jurisdictions that already have structures in place can use the guidebook as a tool to help them improve their structures. Also, jurisdictions that have integrated justice information systems can compare their efforts and ascertain what can be learned from the experiences of other jurisdictions. In addition, this guidebook can be used as a local governance training tool for justice information integration.

Chapter 2
The Need for Integrated Justice Information

The Problem

The U.S. justice system was established to accomplish several purposes: to detect, apprehend, convict, and incarcerate offenders; to deter potential offenders; and to create an ordered society. Its success is immeasurably strengthened when all the components of the justice system have available to them the most current, accurate, and complete data that they can obtain.

The justice system's mission often is hampered or stymied by factors such as

- Inefficient manual processes, disparate or missing data.
- Illegible index cards with seminal crime information.
- Multiple and inconsistent incident/booking reports.
- Uncoordinated relationships among justice agencies.

Offenders have remained free because agencies have not had the capacity to quickly and efficiently communicate with each other. Months, and sometimes years, unfortunately pass before suspects are adjudicated and incarcerated.

The backlog of unprosecuted criminal cases in America continues to grow frighteningly large while, simultaneously, adjudication bodies work at full capacity to keep pace with the layers of bureaucracy that have been created to uphold the principle of due process of the law. Worse still, these barriers trapped criminal justice workers in a recurring cycle of paperwork, filing, and phone calls, resulting in a costly misallocation of safety resources, manual errors, and "lost" work hours that effectively reduce citizen safety. With many of America's local justice agencies relying on sticky notes, faxed messages, undocumented telephone calls, or unsecured e-mail to exchange criminal case information, the integrity, accuracy, and security of that information is at risk.

The end result for all involved has been a slow and expensive judicial process that lacks centralized quality control. For swift, fair, and economical justice to prevail, local governments desperately need a means of managing the integration and automated exchange of key crime information across agency and jurisdictional bounds—a priority of the U.S. Department of Justice since the late 1960s. Early on, law enforcement and Federal Government agencies attempted to encourage information sharing among local jurisdictions by providing funding opportunities through the Law Enforcement Assistance Administration (LEAA) grants.

Paradoxically, these very funds have often contributed to the creation of silos of unshared information. Traditionally, funding from these programs has been "program" or "purpose" specific and unfortunately led to the installation of many different computer systems, in many cases with limited purposes, serving the various justice components in state, local, and tribal governments.

Thirty-plus years have passed since the first LEAA grants were disbursed, with this program having been replaced by the present Community Oriented Policing Services and Local Law Enforcement Block Grant programs. Gaping holes still appear in the achievement of effective local (let alone regional or national) integrated justice information systems. Agencies in the criminal justice system guard information more carefully than any other type of government agency, with the exception, perhaps, of those in national security or the armed forces. Change in bureaucracies that are protective of their data is neither easy nor fast. Despite the inherent complexity of integrating their justice information systems, however, local governments continue to strive to do so in order to expedite justice and improve the safety for their constituents.

Technology Is Only Part of the Solution

Modern advances in computing have the power to drastically change America's justice process. The advent of information technology has had a substantial impact on the way local government agencies integrate and exchange criminal information, thus speeding the processes by which crime is managed, thereby enhancing the capacity of local public safety agencies to respond effectively. Terabit computing systems, scalable data warehouses, improved wire line and wireless telecommunications, and the Internet are already available to foster the exchange of justice information across agencies that need access to real time information. Technology itself is not a panacea for slow and inefficient justice processes. And information systems alone cannot integrate data from one county to another across jurisdictional lines. Such integration of justice information processes and systems requires people in local governments to adapt their processes to such systems. The key to the successful integration of justice information in America's local justice agencies clearly resides with their governance structure.

Well-defined and structured governance empowers the integration of justice information systems because it requires the cooperation of both the community's justice professionals and its elected and appointed officials who possess the detailed process knowledge about their communities that can provide deep and broad perspectives on integration needs. In parallel, governance of integration efforts enables information technology professionals to engineer processes with those who must enforce the rule of law, creating flexible applications that change with the varying needs of the community's police officers, lawyers, judges, jails, and motor vehicle departments. Furthermore, governance structures enable the documentation of the integration process, thus providing a template that other jurisdictions and localities can use in similar efforts. Ultimately, it is governance that consolidates and streamlines the integration of justice information, providing the guidance needed to ensure that technology represents a solution for all those involved in managing the justice system.

The Role of the Federal Government

In 1997, OJP created the Information Technology (IT) Executive Council to help guide federal funding in a more synergistic manner. Through a series of conferences in 1998, the IT Executive Council met with more than 300 representatives from state and local criminal justice systems to

- Determine the stages of justice integration efforts at the state and local levels.
- Identify the issues surrounding the integration of justice information systems.
- Pinpoint the processes that could spur such integration.

The initial meetings took place in February and March of 1998. During the first gathering, a focus group of criminal justice experts from a variety of law enforcement, prosecution, public defense, corrections agencies, and the courts met with the IT Executive Council to discuss how integrated criminal justice information systems are built. As a result, the expert focus group also provided the council with 14 detailed recommendations, including those to

- Structure grants to support the various phases of project development and implementation (research, development, maintenance, etc.).
- Provide a one-stop shop for information, answers, and access to the status of federal standards concerning technology.
- Send federal representatives into the field to help with planning at state and local levels.
- Coordinate state efforts at a national level, work with states to do the same for coordinating local initiatives, and be able to discuss how various federal initiatives work together.

At the March meeting—the Conference of the States—the council met with a contingent of criminal justice representatives from eight states to collect recommendations from the states' point of view. Recommendations stemming from this meeting addressed similar issues:

- Help states conduct regional, state and/or local integration workshops onsite.
- Tie grants to data integrity, security, standards, and planning requirements.
- Recognize that "one size does not fit all."

In July, the council met with criminal justice representatives from an additional 8 states, along with the original 8, and in November met with representatives from 8 more states, along with the original 16. The 1998 conference series provided OJP with the field's recommendations to further state and local justice integration through grant guidance, technical assistance, and the development of a national integration resource center.

At the culmination of this series of meetings, OJP identified the critical first steps needed to help move state and local governments toward the integration of justice information systems. Those eight steps were set forth in OJP's 1999 Integration Initiative:

1. **Building a business case for integration**—Assisting justice information integration efforts by state and local jurisdictions by creating an education and marketing tool for executives, legislators, the judiciary, and the public that demonstrates the value of such integrated systems (currently published; see appendix C: Resources).

2. **A governance initiative**—Examining, at the state level, the governance structures in place and overseeing integration efforts to highlight the strengths and weaknesses of various structures (currently in final review stage).

3. **Procurement improvement initiative**—Rethinking the Office of Federal Procurement Policy process to improve upon it.

4. **Standards initiative**—Surveying and categorizing results to identify current standards and to reach national consensus on technical and data standards for justice integration.

5. **State/local government legislation initiative**—Creating an inventory of legislation that supports integration and that can aid jurisdictions in drafting new or amending current legislation.

6. **Federal Web consortium participation**—OJP joining the consortium to build relationships with other federal agencies, exchange ideas, and work with the agencies on mutually beneficial projects.

7. **Information interchange study**—Studying how information flows through the criminal justice process and how that information is shared.

8. **National Information Resource Center**—Providing a central place for all levels of government pursuing integration efforts to obtain relevant and useful information.

Building upon the progress made during 1999, OJP focused its projects in 2000 on four areas:

- Creating a National Integration Resource Center.
- Facilitating state pilots, initially in Alabama, where OJP is collaborating to build an integrated justice information system in the southwestern portion of the state.
- Helping develop standards for information exchange, maintenance, and architecture development.
- Fostering a justice information privacy initiative that will help states, local governments, and tribal governments.

Overall, OJP-funded information technology initiatives include the following elements:

Functional Standards—OJP is supporting the development of functional standards in the area of courts by the National Center for State Courts (adult criminal and juvenile justice case management systems), the corrections community, and the probation/parole community. In addition, the National Center for State Courts has developed functional standards for civil court case management systems and is planning the development of functional standards for traffic and probate courts.

Resource Center—OJP, through a cooperative agreement with REI Systems Inc., will create a Web page to support state and local government teams responsible for developing integrated justice information systems. OJP will populate the Web page with content based on recommendations from a Justice Practitioners Working Group and will task the National Center for Rural Law Enforcement to help consolidate the recommended content.

XML Initiative—OJP sponsored a workshop in March 2001 that brought together teams responsible for implementing leading edge applications of XML used to facilitate exchange of information among courts, the intelligence community, and the criminal record history community. Workshop discussions will be used to determine the appropriate role that OJP should play in coordinating the development and implementation of XML applications in the justice community.

Industry Working Group—OJP is working with the private sector through an Industry Working Group to obtain its views on planned policy and implementation initiatives and its recommendations to improve government approaches to procurement reform, technology refreshment, standards, and software development. OJP also is examining the feasibility of tasking a nonprofit spinoff of the Working Group to provide technology assistance and periodic seminars on emerging technologies.

Governance Studies—OJP has been working with the National Criminal Justice Association on a state survey to identify and document the characteristics of governance models across the country that oversee the development and implementation of integrated criminal justice systems. Similarly, OJP is partnering with PTI on a local government survey to identify and document characteristics of local governance models used to operate integrated justice systems in counties, municipalities, and regional units of government. The latter project is this guidebook.

Indian Nations—OJP has been working in partnership with the Office of Tribal Justice to facilitate the planning, design, and implementation of integrated information systems by various Indian Nations. In particular OJP has supported an effort to share justice information among the Navajo, Hopi, Zuni, and other tribal nations in the United States. OJP is also supporting plans by the Navajo Nation to conduct a Summit on Integration for their tribe.

Privacy—OJP is implementing a three-part program aimed at improving privacy in the development and implementation of justice information systems. The first initiative resulted in the creation of *Privacy Design Principles for an Integrated Justice System*. This was followed by the development of a *Privacy Impact Assessment for Justice Information Systems*. These documents are available on the OJP Integrated Justice Web page (www.ojp.usdoj.gov/integratedjustice). The third and final initiative is a series of three workshops aimed at producing guidelines for Public Access to Criminal Justice Electronic Records. OJP and the Bureau of Justice Statistics are planning to task The SEARCH Group, Inc. to schedule a national conference on privacy later this year to roll out some of the products produced by this initiative.

Courts—OJP is also supporting state courts through partnerships with the National Center for State Courts and affiliated organizations (including the Conference of State Court Administrators, the National Association of Court Management, and the Conference of Chief Justices). Partnership efforts include providing technical assistance to the courts, support tools for small and rural courts, developing functional standards for case management systems, and a Web crawler capability to facilitate information gathering from state court administration Web pages.

Legislation—OJP, in partnership with the National Conference of State Legislators, is working to identify legislative initiatives affecting the justice community and to elevate the understanding of integration and information sharing issues on the part of state legislators.

Architecture—OJP and the National Association of State Chief Information Officers are working to conceptualize and implement appropriate architectures, frameworks, and information sharing standards to facilitate the movement of justice information across jurisdictional boundaries. PTI is considering similar efforts with an organization representing local governments.

Project Management—With assistance from the Industry Working Group, OJP, the University of New Orleans Center for Society, Law and Justice, and Auburn University have developed a curriculum aimed at educating and certifying state and local officials in technology project management.

State Strategic Planning—OJP and the National Governors Association (NGA) are conducting a series of workshops designed to develop implementation plans for integration of justice information systems. OJP has funded the travel for participating states to attend the workshops and prepare implementation plans. This initiative is designed to involve the governors of states more personally and to provide incentives for competing for additional implementation grants. Funding will be based on competitive review of states' plans by NGA and an advisory board established by NGA.

Business Case—OJP funded the development of guidance to state and local governments for the preparation of business case concepts to help them secure resources and leadership support for integration and information sharing. The Center for Technology in Government developed guidelines based on workshop input from elected and appointed executives and leaders from the criminal justice community. The guideline document is available on the OJP Web site (www.ojp.usdoj.gov/integratedjustice).

Information Exchange Points—OJP and The SEARCH Group are identifying and documenting key points at which justice information is transferred between jurisdictions. A computerized model is being developed to illustrate the flow of information and demonstrate optimal exchange conditions to facilitate the development of appropriate standards for integration.

Strategic Planning Model—OJP funded the development of a Strategic Planning Model by the International Association of Chiefs of Police (IACP). The documented version of this product is available from IACP and will be placed on the OJP Resource Center Web page upon completion.

Technology Standards—OJP has funded the development of a process for identifying, selecting, and approving technology standards for use by the justice community. The project was developed by the Office of Law Enforcement Standards, National Center for Law Enforcement and Corrections Technology Centers, and the National Telecommunications and Information Administration through the National Institute of Justice.

Corrections—OJP is exploring the possibility of partnering with the Corrections Technology Association to develop functional standards for the corrections community.

Law Enforcement Intelligence—OJP is sponsoring the quarterly meeting of the Law Enforcement Intelligence Forum to recommend appropriate processes, standards and policies for improving the management of intelligence information by the law enforcement community.

Transportation Systems—OJP is partnering with the U.S. Department of Transportation to create a Public Safety Program within the transportation community designed to create synergy between public safety and transportation initiatives. A memorandum of understanding (MOU) committing both departments to support their respective information sharing efforts was recently signed.

Justice Integration Earmarks—OJP will be monitoring initiatives established by Congress as earmarks for projects to implement integrated justice information systems. Examples of this type of project include those earmarked for the eastern part of Kentucky and the Southwestern Alabama Project.

Coordination—OJP coordinated meetings in April 2001 for grantees and technical assistance providers to exchange information about their programs and to learn about the overall program envisioned by OJP.

Technical Assistance—OJP is working with various organizations to provide technical assistance to the justice community on a broad basis. Some of the organizations involved include: The SEARCH Group; the University of Arkansas Criminal Justice Institute and its National Center for Rural Law Enforcement; the University of New Orleans Center for Society, Law and Justice; the National Center for State Courts; the

Institute for Intergovernmental Research; the Community Oriented Policing Services; the Development Services Group; the Center for Network Development; the National Criminal Justice Association; and the National Institute of Corrections.

PTI's Role

During the course of meetings held in 1999, OJP discovered the importance of governance structures in cities and counties to oversee the integration of justice information systems at the local level. To help OJP, PTI proposed developing a guide to governance from the local government perspective. PTI's role was to examine local governance structures to determine their types, qualities, and capabilities. Through a cooperative agreement with OJP, PTI studied current and planned governance structures of cities and counties for the integration of justice information systems.

PTI conducted a national survey of local government elected and appointed officials to ascertain their efforts to integrate justice information systems, types of governance structures in place to facilitate integration, and how those structures were created. The survey also was designed to identify those jurisdictions that were engaged in integrating systems and/or have governance structures to facilitate this integration. The survey results have been compiled, and the analysis of the findings serves as the foundation for this guidebook.

Chapter 3
Status of Integration and Governance Structures To Facilitate Integration

Operation of Integrated Information Systems

Initially, survey respondents were asked about the status of justice information system integration in their jurisdictions. Questions focused on integration efforts among departments/agencies, with other local jurisdictions and with state criminal justice information systems. Three-quarters of survey respondents reported that their jurisdictions operate integrated information systems with other departments/agencies (see Figure 4).

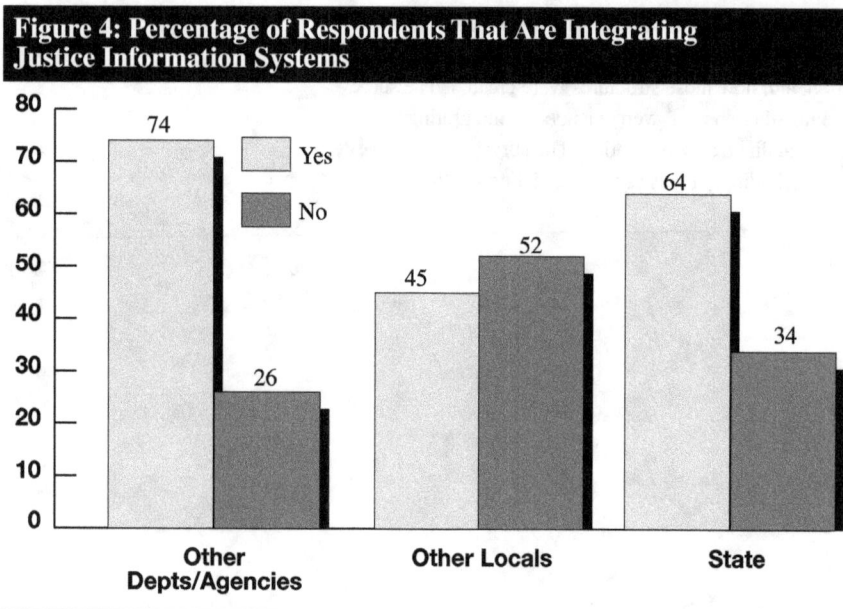

Figure 4: Percentage of Respondents That Are Integrating Justice Information Systems

Note: Percentages do not total 100% because there were some who did not respond to the question.

Clearly, respondents were more likely to be involved in integration within their jurisdictions (74%) than with other local jurisdictions (45%) or with state systems (64%). A greater percentage of larger jurisdictions indicated they are integrated with other jurisdictions than did smaller jurisdictions. Only 38% of jurisdictions with populations of less than 50,000 were integrated with other jurisdictions, while 55% of those with populations of more than 50,000 were integrated with other jurisdictions. Differences based on size of population were less pronounced in responses relating to integration with state criminal justice information systems.

Regardless of the type of integration (among departments/agencies or with other local jurisdictions), justice systems that were most likely to be integrated were law enforcement, emergency communications, courts, and the department of motor vehicles. Of the non-justice systems, a greater percentage of the agencies within jurisdictions were integrated with planning/zoning (22%), public works (19%), and public utilities (12%). Outside their jurisdiction, more agencies were integrated with planning/zoning (20%) and transportation (17%).

More than half of the participants (55%) had implemented public access rules, while only about one-fifth had developed an integrated information technology strategic plan (21%). Larger jurisdictions with populations of more than 50,000 were more likely to have public access rules (55% v. 38%) and a technology strategic plan (33% v. 10%).

Description of Justice Integration Efforts and Governance Structures

Respondents were asked to place their jurisdictions in one of four categories best describing current justice integration efforts:

1. No justice integration effort underway nor a governance structure to facilitate such integration.
2. A governance structure to facilitate the integration of the justice information systems, but no current integration of systems.
3. Justice information systems integration, but no governance structure in place.
4. Justice information systems integration and a governance structure in place.

The largest percentage of respondents (34%) fell into the first category: no integration, no governance structure, while the smallest percentage (12%) had a governance structure but no current systems integration (see figure 5). The responses based on the status of their integration are reported in the following three chapters. More detail on each of these four categories is presented in the following chapters.

Figure 5: Status of Integration/Governance Structure

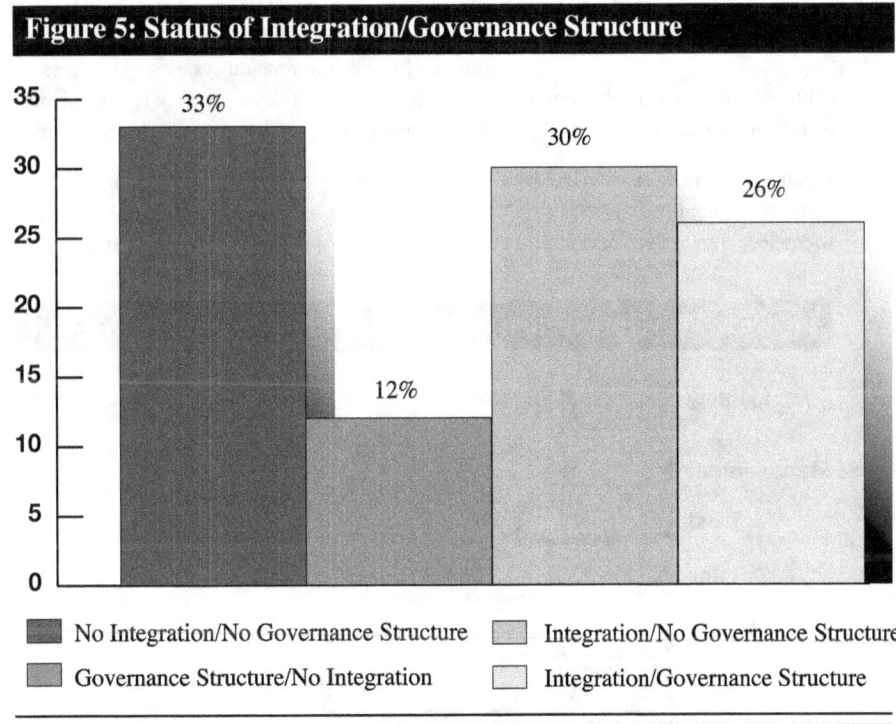

Legend:
- No Integration/No Governance Structure
- Governance Structure/No Integration
- Integration/No Governance Structure
- Integration/Governance Structure

Chapter 4
No Justice Integration/
No Governance Structure

When jurisdictions were compared by population size, there was a significant variance between the percentage of jurisdictions in the sample and the ones reporting no integration/no governance structure (see table 1). For example, the larger areas, jurisdictions with populations of more than 250,000, made up 20% of the sample, but only 8% of the jurisdictions with no integration and no governance structure. Jurisdictions with populations between 10,000 and 50,000 made up 38% of the sample, but they were almost half of the jurisdictions with no integration or governance structure.

Table 1: Comparison of Jurisdictions by Percent of Sample Size and Percent of Jurisdictions With No Integration/No Governance Structure

Population	% Of Sample	% With No Integration No Governance	Difference
< 10,000	13	18	+5
10,000–50,000	38	49	+11
50,000–100,000	14	12	-2
100,000–250,000	14	12	-2
250,000+	20	8	-12

Why Agencies Are Not Engaged in Integration

Respondents were provided with nine preselected options (although they could write in a response) to explain why their jurisdictions were not engaged in the integration of justice information systems: (1) politics, (2) power/control, (3) data/information security, (4) size of relevant agency(ies), (5) liability, (6) trust, (7) agency "cultural" issues, (8) funding, and (9) risk management/exposure.

Funding was the most often cited reason (26%) for not engaging in integrated justice systems (see figure 6). Data security was selected by 15%, and size of relevant agency(ies) was selected by 14%. The majority of respondents (82%) who were not engaged in

Figure 6: Why Jurisdiction Not Engaged in Integration (in percentages)

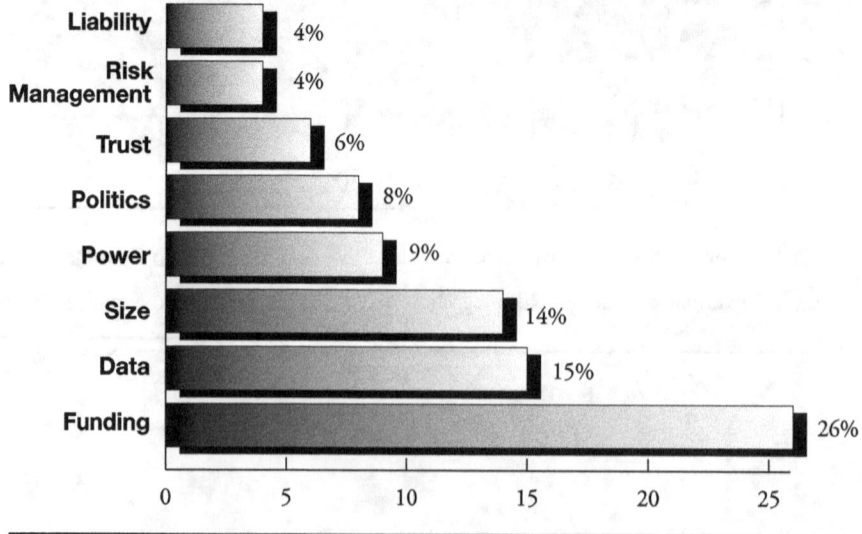

Liability	4%
Risk Management	4%
Trust	6%
Politics	8%
Power	9%
Size	14%
Data	15%
Funding	26%

integration nor had a governance structure reported that they had not attempted integration in the past. Those that had attempted to integrate justice information systems but were unsuccessful were asked to describe their experience and explain why their efforts had failed. Lack of funding was the major reason given, but other reasons included agency incompatibility and politics.

Respondents were given a list of 13 barriers, and were required to select those that were preventing the integration of their jurisdictions' justice information systems (see table 2). Lack of funding was selected by far more agencies than any other barrier. A number of jurisdictions responded that the size of their jurisdiction and/or budget prevented them from integrating. Secondary barriers were staffing/personnel and technology issues. The personnel barrier was related to the funding barrier because jurisdictions were likely to state that they could not afford the personnel needed for an integrated system. Similarly, several jurisdictions tied their technology issues to funding problems.

Why Jurisdictions Had Not Established a Governance Structure

When asked why they had not established a governance structure, the responses were similar to those given for not integrating (see figure 6). Funding was cited by 28%, size was selected by 16%, and data/information security was selected by 13% (see figure 7). Politics was identified as the reason for no governance structure by 12%. This was less than the 8% that identified politics as the reason that they were not engaged in integration. Data/information security was more of a limitation in the larger jurisdictions (250,000+ population) than it was in the smaller jurisdictions. Twenty-six percent of the respondents from larger jurisdictions listed data security as a barrier compared to only

Table 2: Barriers to Integration

Barriers	Number	Percent
Funding	64	21.0
Lack of Champion	15	4.9
Political	21	6.9
Lack of Governance Structure	15	4.9
Staffing/Personnel	35	11.5
Turf Issues	27	8.9
Size of Agency	19	6.2
Liability	12	3.9
Data Security	25	8.2
Trust	8	2.6
Cultural Issue	9	3.0
Technology Issues	31	10.2
Risk Management/ Exposure	14	4.6

Figure 7: Why Governance Structure Not Established

Category	Value
Other	12.7
Agency Culture	1.7
Trust	4.6
Liability	5.2
Power/Control	8.7
Politics	11.6
Data	13.3
Size	15.5
Funding	27.7

7% of those with 50,000–100,000 population and 11% of those with populations of 100,000–250,000.

Of those jurisdictions without a governance structure, 85% had not attempted to establish a governance structure to facilitate integration. The 15% that had tried and failed in their attempts to establish a governance structure attributed the failure to funding. A number of other respondents blamed the failure on politics.

What Would Be Included in an Integrated System?

When asked what agencies would likely be included if their jurisdictions were to integrate their justice information systems, 15% indicated that law enforcement would be included, 11% would include the courts, 10% would include the prosecutor, and 10% would include emergency communications. Agencies that elicited the fewest responses were transportation (0.6%), the health department (0.8%), the public defender (1.4%), and social services (1.6%).

Outside Assistance Needed

Respondents identified disparate types of assistance needed from the federal, state, local, and regional levels of government (see table 3). The type of assistance most desired from the federal and state governments was funding, while personnel/staff was the assistance most desired from the local level (15%). Forty percent of the respondents felt that federal funding would help their jurisdictions engage in justice integration, while 22% selected state funding. This compares with only 11% who felt that local funding would help, and 13% who felt that regional funding would help. Besides funding, federal assistance was needed in strategic planning (10%) and facilitation (10%). Fifteen percent of the respondents wanted strategic planning from their state or region. Consultant assistance was cited by 12% and 11%, respectively, from their state and region. The local government and the region were viewed as the most helpful sources in assisting with operation and management planning and in developing public/private partnerships.

Table 3: Percentage of Outside Assistance That Would Help With Integration				
Type of Assistance	Federal	State	Regional	Local
Funding	41.0	22.3	13.4	11.4
Strategic Planning	10.1	14.5	14.6	11.7
Implementation	7.0	10.8	11.8	13.2
Facilitation	10.1	10.8	11.0	9.4
Consultants	8.9	13.0	11.4	8.8
Industry	3.2	4.5	5.7	5.3
Staff/Personnel	5.7	7.4	8.1	14.9
Marketing Plan	5.1	6.7	7.7	6.4
Operation & Management Plans/Budgeting	4.4	7.4	10.6	12.0
Public/Private Partnership	2.5	1.5	4.5	6.1
Other	1.9	1.1	1.2	.9

Governance Structure With No Integration

Twelve percent of the respondents indicated that they have established a governance structure to facilitate the integration of their justice information systems but are currently not doing so (see figure 5). Of the jurisdictions in this category, the smallest percentage was found in rural areas (10%), while the largest (41%) was in urban areas. In examining geographical types, it was revealed that only a small percentage of each type had a governance structure with no integration: rural areas (6%), suburban areas (12%), and urban areas (14%).

When jurisdictions were compared by population size, less than one-fourth of each of the geographical types of jurisdictions had a governance structure. The largest percentage (20%), was from jurisdictions with a population of more than 250,000. Jurisdictions with populations of more than 250,000 were most disproportionate to their sample percentage (see table 4), meaning the frequency of their having a governance structure with no integration was higher than their sample proportionality in the survey would have predicted.

Origin, Nature and Functions of Governance Structures

The largest number of jurisdictions (44%) had a governance structure that was formed through a cooperative agreement, memorandum of understanding, or some similar document. Some structures were created by statute (15%), others were loose configurations with informal guidelines (11%), and still others were established as a grant requirement (8%).

Affected personnel initiated the governance structure for 47% of the jurisdictions (see table 6). Fourteen percent of respondents stated their structures were begun as the result of a legislative mandate.

State Integration Efforts

When questioned about state-level justice information system integration, most respondents did not know the status of their states' efforts (63%). Of those who did know about their states' efforts, 57% said their states were engaged in integration planning, while 43% said their states did not have integration efforts underway.

Those whose states were engaged in integration were asked how they learned about the effort. Close to one-third (32%) stated their agencies were notified, 18% indicated their jurisdictions were notified, and 18% responded that their jurisdictions were invited to the table. Less than half of the jurisdictions that knew about their states' efforts (40%) were participating.

Summary Points

- Funding is a major impediment to the integration of justice information systems and the establishment of governance structures.
- Law enforcement, the courts, prosecutors, and emergency communications are the key agencies to include in an integrated system.
- The type of assistance needed from a local government may differ from the assistance needed from the federal and state governments.

Table 4: Comparison of Jurisdictions by Percent of Survey Sample and Percent of Jurisdictions *With* a Governance Structure/*No* Integration

Population	% of Sample	% With Governance Structure/No Integration	Difference
10,000	13	3	-10
10,000-50,000	38	41	+3
50,000-100,000	14	3	11
100,000-250,000	14	17	+3
250,000+	20	35	+15

Table 5: Comparison of Jurisdictions by Percent of Survey Sample and Percent of Jurisdictions *With* a Governance Structure *and* Justice Integration

Population	% of Sample	% With Governance Structure/Integration	Difference
10,000	13	9	-4
10,000–50,000	38	28	-10
50,000–100,000	14	22	+8
100,000–250,000	14	12	-2
250,000+	20	26	+6

Table 6: How the Governance Structure Was Initiated

How Structure Initiated	Number	Percent
Created for another purpose	9	9.8
Legislative mandate	13	14.1
By affected personnel	43	46.7
By key advocate/champion	13	14.1
Other	13	14.1

Chapter 5
Governance Structure
With or Without Integration

Governance Structure With Integration

One-fourth (26%) of the respondents have a governance structure in place and are integrating justice information systems (see Figure 5). Of the jurisdictions in this category, the largest percentage (42%) was in urban areas, 25% were from the suburbs, and 17% were in rural areas. The following percentage of each type had a governance structure with integration: rural areas (23%), suburban areas (14%), and urban areas (32%).

When population was used to compare jurisdictions with governance and integration, jurisdictions with populations of 250,000+ and jurisdictions with populations from 50,000 to 100,000 were the only population types in the plus column, i.e., their percentage of jurisdictions with governance and integration was greater than their percentage of the sample (see table 5).

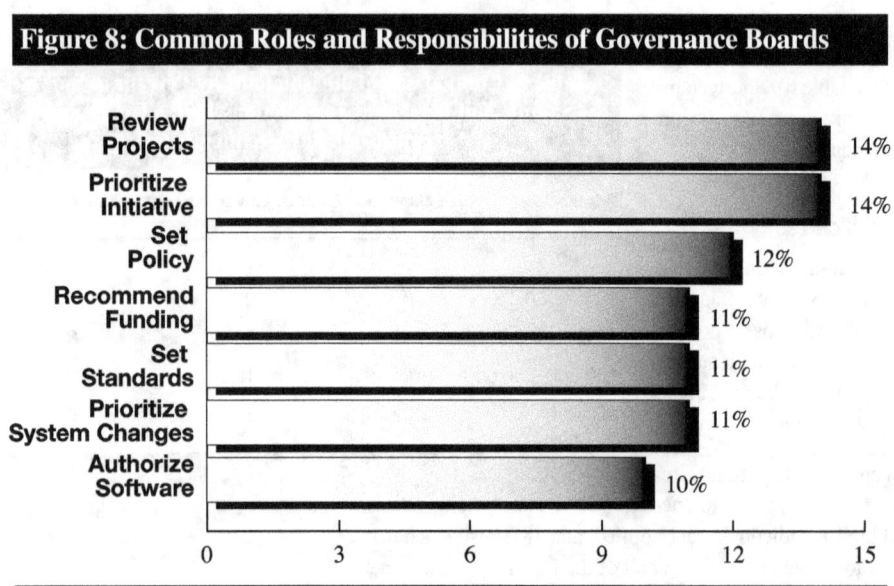

Figure 8: Common Roles and Responsibilities of Governance Boards

Law enforcement was identified as the most important agency for participation in the governance structure. More than one-fifth of the jurisdictions (21%) indicated that law enforcement participates in their governance structures. The courts participate in 12%, the prosecutor participates in 11%, and the central information technology agency is a part of 10% of the structures.

Members of the governance body were more likely to be appointed than to be elected or selected through some other method. It was reported that most governance bodies did not have their own staff (39%), and that the reporting entities for these bodies varied based on form of government (i.e., mayor/council, city/county manager, county executive/commission).

Respondents were asked to identify the roles and responsibilities of their governance board from among nine options. The most common roles were to review projects (14%), prioritize initiatives (14%), set policy (12%), recommend funding (11%), set standards (11%), prioritize system changes (11%), and authorize software (10%) (see figure 8).

Less than half of the governance structures (40%) have fiscal authority. Most of the ones with fiscal authority have spending authority (88%) but no taxing authority (12%).

Involvement of local elected officials in the governance structure is varied. One-fourth of the respondents indicated that their local elected officials participate in the governance structure. Other respondents indicated lower levels of participation for such functions as funding (21%) and mandating the structure (14%). Fifteen percent of the respondents stated that their local officials were not aware of the structure. One-third or more of the smallest jurisdictions (10,000 or less population) and jurisdictions with populations of 50,000 to 100,000 indicated that their local elected officials participate in the governance structure. Approximately one-fourth of all the other jurisdictions indicated that their local officials participate in the governance structure, except those with populations from 10,000 to 50,000. Only 14% of these jurisdictions reported participation by their local officials. Nevertheless, only 14% of jurisdictions with populations from 10,000 to 50,000 indicated that their officials were not aware of the structure. This compares to one-third of the jurisdictions with less than 10,000 population and one-fifth of those with population sizes from 50,000 to 250,000.

Funding for Governance Structures

Most respondents had not received outside funding for their governance body (see figure 9). Only 11% had received federal block grants, while 14% had received state funding. Over one-third indicated their governance bodies are funded out of their normal operating budgets, and 17% stated that their governance bodies are not funded. When population size was taken into consideration, it was found that the smaller jurisdictions were more likely to be funded by federal or state funds (43%) than the largest jurisdictions (13%).

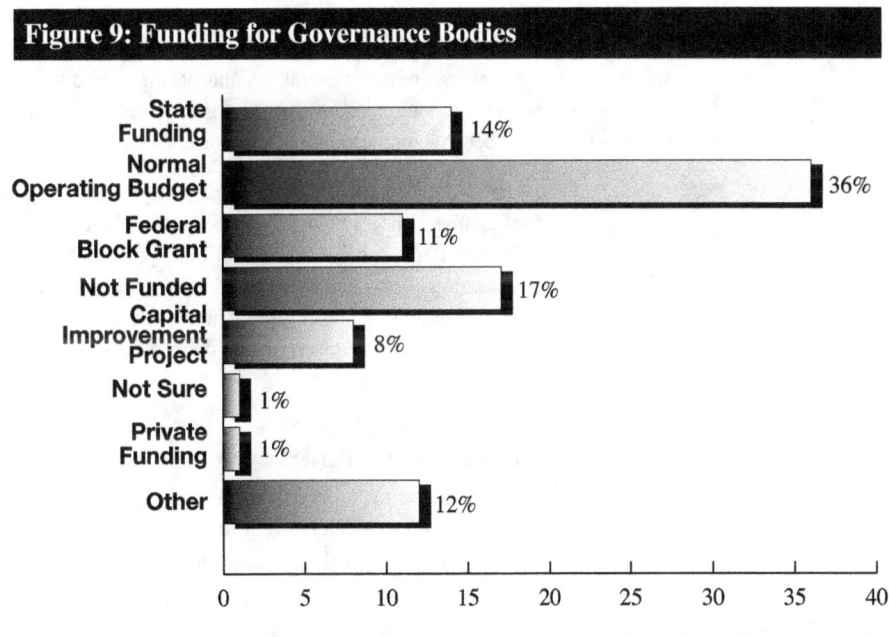

Figure 9: Funding for Governance Bodies

Several jurisdictions had unique mechanisms for funding their governance structures. One had an add-on fee, another used a pool of federal grant funds to individual jurisdictions, and still another had a CRT Enhancement Fund. Although a few jurisdictions had seen an increase in funding, most still had funding concerns.

Involvement in Federal and State Integration Efforts

When asked about the involvement of their jurisdictions' governance bodies in federal justice integration efforts, 42% stated their jurisdictions had received federal grants. Only

11% were actively involved in the NCIC (National Crime Information Center) 2000 changes, and 21% of respondents were unaware of federal justice information system integration efforts.

Involvement by local governance bodies in statewide justice information system integration was both voluntary and mandated. One-third of the jurisdictions were invited to voluntarily participate in statewide efforts, and 13% had been mandated to participate. Unlike federal involvement, only 3% of respondents were involved in statewide integration through a state grant. Thirteen percent of those who were aware of their states' efforts were not participating; 18% were not aware of any state integration efforts. The percentage of respondents unaware of their states' integration efforts increased to 25% when the responses of the jurisdictions with governance structures were separated from those without governance structures.

Factors Having a Positive/Negative Impact on the Governance Structure

When asked to list the factors that had a positive impact on their governance structures, a variety of responses was given. However, one common theme was found in many of the responses—the structure benefited from cooperation between the jurisdictions involved. Funding, especially state and federal funding, was considered to have a positive impact by many respondents. Several respondents mentioned the impact of good leadership and commitment. These factors were suggested because they have created more efficiency, facilitated better communication between agencies, and forged a spirit of working together.

One theme was consistent throughout many of the responses concerning factors that have a negative impact on governance structures: lack of funding. Other prominent themes were staff shortage, political agendas or other political factors, and changes in personnel or leadership. A few mentioned inadequate infrastructures or equipment, competition, and lack of agreement on priorities. One respondent summed up the sentiment expressed by many: "All of these place a strain on resources and encourage competition rather than cooperation."

Summary Points

- Governance structures tend to be started by agreements such as memoranda of understanding and by the people most affected by the structures.
- Law enforcement is the key agency for participation in a governance structure.
- Some of the key functions of governance structures are reviewing projects, prioritizing initiatives, setting policies, and setting standards.
- Governance structures tend to be funded by local funds.
- Governance structures bring about better cooperation between agencies.
- Lack of funding impedes the development of governance structures.

Thirty percent of respondents were engaged in integrating justice information systems but had no governance structure in place (see figure 5). Ten percent of the jurisdictions in this category were located in rural areas, 37% in urban areas, 40% in suburban areas, and 14% did not indicate where they were located. The data was examined to determine what percentage of each type of jurisdiction had integration but no governance structure. The results indicated that one-third of the suburban respondents and 32% of the urban areas were integrating without a governance structure. A smaller percentage of the rural areas, 15%, had achieved integration without a governance structure.

Table 7: Comparison of Jurisdictions by Percent of Survey Sample and Percent of Jurisdictions *With* Integration and *No* Governance Structure

Population	% of Sample	% With Integration/ No Governance Structure	Difference
10,000	13	15	+2
10,000-50,000	38	33	-5
50,000-100,000	14	14	0
100,000-250,000	14	16	+2
250,000+	20	22	+2

Little variance was found between the percentage of jurisdictions in the sample and the ones reporting integration but no governance structure when jurisdictions were compared by population size (see table 7). For example, the larger areas, jurisdictions with populations of more than 250,000, made up 20% of the sample and 22% of the jurisdictions with no integration and no governance structure. Jurisdictions with populations from 50,000 to 100,000 made up 14% of the sample, and they were 14% of the jurisdictions with no integration or governance structure. When integration involved state agencies, the office of public safety/state police was most likely to be included. A number of jurisdictions also indicated integration with the department of motor vehicles (16%), and the bureau of criminal identification (12%). Few jurisdictions were integrating with private or media groups (6%). Integration tends to operate with a bidirectional data flow (48%) or with a single point of entry (27%). Few jurisdictions have a one-way data flow (8%).

Chapter 6
Integration Without a Governance Structure

Barriers to Integration

Funding was, by far, the most common barrier to integration cited by respondents (see table 9). Other identified barriers were technology issues (15%), staffing/personnel (14%), turf issues (14%), and political issues (11%). Funding, however, was not selected as the number one barrier by the smallest jurisdictions. For jurisdictions of less than 10,000, technology issues were the top impediment.

Table 8: Type of Integration		
Type of Integration	**Number**	**Percent**
Within single agency	22	16.7
Between agencies within the jurisdiction	37	28.0
Between agencies outside jurisdictions or regionally	52	39.4
Between agencies of jurisdictions across state boundary	19	14.4
Other	2	1.5

Origin and Nature of Integration

More than one-fourth (26%) of the jurisdictions' justice integration processes were started by top staff. Almost as many were started by a grassroots effort (21%). Others were begun with an interlocal agreement (18%), a federal/state grant (10%), statutory mandate (5%), and an advisory group/association (4%). When the data was analyzed by population size, it was found that a greater percentage of structures in jurisdictions with less than 10,000 population was started by interlocal agreements, and a greater percentage of structures in jurisdictions of 250,000 population or more was started by grassroots efforts.

The largest number of jurisdictions (40%) were involved in integration with agencies outside their jurisdictions or with agencies within their jurisdiction (28%) (see table 8). A much smaller number (14% and 16%, respectively) were integrating across state boundaries or with a single agency.

Table 9: Barriers to Integration		
Barriers	**Number**	**Percent**
Funding	59	24.7
Political Issues	25	10.5
Lack of Strategic Planning	22	9.2
Lack of Support	10	4.2
Turf Issues	33	13.8
Technology Issues	36	15.1
Lack of Governance Structure	16	6.7
Staffing/Personnel	33	13.8
Other	5	2.1

Would a Governance Structure Benefit Integration?

Respondents were asked if they thought a governance structure would benefit their justice information systems integration efforts. Whereas 73% of all respondents felt that a governance structure would benefit their integration efforts, 38% of those without a governance structure did not feel that having one necessarily would benefit their jurisdiction (see figure 10). On the other hand, 90% of those with governance structures stated that the structure furthered their integration efforts.

When asked why they did not feel that a structure would benefit their integration, many respondents stated they were doing well without a structure.

They were concerned about changes should a structure be superimposed over their current activities. Their concerns revolved around issues such as the politics of the structure, whether more bureaucracy would be required, and potential restrictions or controls.

Respondents who felt that a structure would benefit their integration efforts identified some of its advantages as better coordination, standardization, and set guidelines or policies. Other benefits suggested were better communication and more funding opportunities. Some felt that a structure would help reduce or eliminate turf battles.

When governance structure exists, other organizations fulfill critical roles. Forty-seven percent of the jurisdictions having no governance structure use an individual agency to implement their integration efforts. A centralized information technology department is in charge in 29% of the jurisdictions, and an interagency body coordinates in 10% of jurisdictions.

Funding for Integration Efforts

For 31% of jurisdictions, funding for the initial procurement and implementation of the integrated justice information system came from their normal operating budgets, not from grants. However, federal grants were an initial source of funding for 21%, while state funding provided initial procurement and implementation for 14%. Private funding was not a factor in providing initial capital, as not one jurisdiction in this category reported receiving private funds. An initial source of funding for 14% of the jurisdictions in this category was capital improvement funds.

When respondents were questioned on funding for ongoing integrated justice system operation, a large percentage (44%) reported their operating budget as the source of funds,

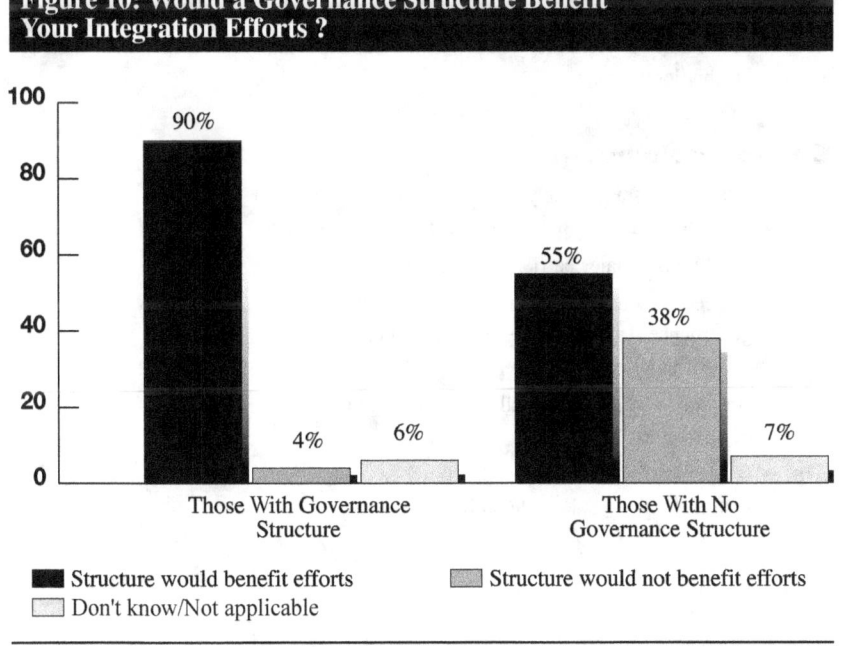

Figure 10: Would a Governance Structure Benefit Your Integration Efforts ?

Those With Governance Structure — 90%, 4%, 6%
Those With No Governance Structure — 55%, 38%, 7%

■ Structure would benefit efforts   ▨ Structure would not benefit efforts
▢ Don't know/Not applicable

Table 10: Agencies Involved in Integration Within Jurisdiction		
Agencies	**Number**	**Percent**
Law enforcement	65	36.9
Prosecution	24	13.6
Courts	33	18.8
Public Defender	1	.6
Corrections	21	11.9
Probation	13	7.4
Parole	7	4.0
Other	12	6.8

with state and federal funding, as well as capital improvement funds, playing smaller roles (12%, 10%, and 8%, respectively). Ten percent of the respondents reported that user fees help to fund their ongoing operations.

The normal operating budget also was most often selected (38%) when respondents were asked about sources of funding. Law enforcement is the primary agency involved in justice information system integration, whether the integration is between agencies within a jurisdiction or among agencies outside the jurisdiction. Within jurisdictions, law enforcement (37%), the courts (19%), prosecution (14%) and corrections (12%) were the agencies most respondents identified for enhancement/improvements to their systems. Federal grants were used by 17% of the respondents, the capital improvement budget by 12%, and state funding resources by 12%. Agencies involved in integration, as identified by respondents, included law enforcement (40%), the courts (19%), corrections (12%), prosecution (14%), probation (7%), and parole (4%) (see table 10).

Jurisdictions face a variety of funding challenges in securing funds for integrated criminal justice technologies. Many respondents stated that finding the funds to support their integration efforts was one of their biggest challenges. Other challenges listed were competition for such funds once they were identified, justifying the need for funds to policymakers, budget limitations, and the cost of maintaining and upgrading systems. Some of the challenges listed related directly to grants, such as finding matching funds, paperwork, not enough grant sources or overall funding levels, and complicated application processes. Despite all the challenges mentioned, some jurisdictions have adopted unique mechanisms for funding their systems. Some of the mechanisms listed were dedicated CRT enhancement, annexation fees, set-asides from county filing fees, asset seizures, voter-approved sales tax, capital outlay technology improvement fund, pooled grant funding, and state-approved technology fees.

Summary Points

- Integration is most likely to be started by top staff, as a grassroots effort, or by an interlocal agency agreement.
- Funding is a major barrier to integration.
- Concerns about changes that would result from having a governance structure may prevent jurisdictions from establishing them.
- An individual agency usually takes the lead in the absence of a structure.
- Integration tends to be funded out of local budgets, but grants play a big role in the initiation of some systems.

Chapter 7
Case Studies

The case studies discussed in this chapter provide snapshots of the governance structures and justice integration efforts in six localities. The site visit team selected these jurisdictions based on the nature of their survey responses, their population, demographics, the type of governance structure being used or explored; and the sort of justice information integration effort already underway or being planned.

HENNEPIN COUNTY, MINNESOTA

Scenario

Hennepin and Dakota Counties share the distinction of being the only two counties in Minnesota that were awarded state grants in 1999 to integrate justice information systems. Hennepin's Criminal Justice System Information Integration Project (CJSIIP) began in 1999 and was originally planned to address integration needs only within the county. The CJSIIP evolved, however, into a project that would build a local model for criminal justice information integration statewide. Hennepin's CJSIIP was analyzed in Dakota County to see if the state's blueprint for criminal justice integration would work in a more rural county. To fund efforts for the CJSIIP, the state awarded Hennepin County a $500,000 grant, which is part of Minnesota's CriMNet initiative for constructing a statewide justice information network.

According to a member of the PTI site visit team, Hennepin and Dakota counties' integration projects are horizontal, involving justice agencies from other jurisdictions or agencies. The goal of the CJSIIP is to integrate law enforcement information systems with adjudication, prosecution and detention systems, creating a systems architecture that makes information available to individuals and agencies along any point of the criminal justice spectrum.

"We're integrating all the criminal-justice information systems in Hennepin County," said Ron Wiborg, contracts and grants manager of the county's Department of Community Corrections, and a member of the PTI working group. "In Minnesota, the county is totally responsible for pre- and post-trial detention, prosecution, probation, and parole. The state operates the court system; all judges, court administrators and all employees in the court administrator's office are, or soon will be, state employees.

"More than 40 law enforcement agencies are in the county, including the county sheriff," he continued. "But we have one corrections system, one prosecutorial system and one court system. One single agency handles all of corrections. One single agency (the county attorney's office) prosecutes all felony and gross misdemeanor offenses and there is one court system. The fragmentation—the dispersion of the parts of the system—really only applies to law enforcement."

The goal is to create an information network from which one agency can access another agency's justice information system in real time; accomplishing that goal is just around the corner. Still, just getting to this point has taken some time. Minnesota's legislature enacted statutes that created the environment in which such a project could flourish by giving counties legal authority and funding to launch an integration solution.

Wiborg explained, "The need for a state oversight committee was obvious, but the legislature also recognized that it should not fill that role. An oversight committee was statutorily created, housed in the state court administrator's office, and directed to develop and implement a statewide criminal justice information network." Because Hennepin County's criminal justice system is the state's largest and most complex, it will be the first integrated system developed.

Another key component to the integration effort has been the private sector, especially a group known as Minnesota HEALS (Hope, Education And Law and Safety), which was started by Honeywell (whose world headquarters resided in Minneapolis at the time) and the Minnesota Business Partnership. The partnership is a group of the 100 largest corporations in the state, many of which had gone through massive systems integration themselves to improve internal business processes. The executive director of the partnership successfully explained to the state legislature the complexity of integrating information systems and demonstrated how applying corporate "best practices" could aid the state in its goal of achieving an integrated criminal justice information system.

Governance Structure

Hennepin County's Criminal Justice Coordinating Committee (CJCC) was formally established in 1998 as a forum through which local units of government in Hennepin County may, by association, consultation, and study, cooperatively promote improvements in the criminal justice system that transcend departments, agencies, and the geographical boundaries of the individual communities. The CJCC, which operated for 12 years informally before 1998, was a natural fit to implement the CJSIIP (see figure 11).

Figure 11: Membership of the CJCC

Hennepin County Board of Commissioners (two members)
Hennepin County Suburban Mayor (one member)
Hennepin County Sheriff
Hennepin County Attorney
Hennepin County Director of Community Corrections
Mayor of Minneapolis
Minneapolis City Council (two members)
City Attorney Office
Minneapolis Police Chief
Chief Judge of the District Court
Presiding Judge of the Juvenile Court
Fourth Judicial District Court Administrator
Fourth Judicial District Public Defender
Hennepin County Suburban Police Chief (one member)

The CJCC oversees the county's justice integration effort, and the county's IT committee handles the actual implementation of the effort. The CJCC created the Integrated Systems Advisory Board (ISAB) to make recommendations for projects that contribute to integration of justice information systems (see figure 12). The ISAB is comprised of representatives from the state, Hennepin County, Minneapolis, and members of the Local Government Information Systems Association. According to the CJCC document that created ISAB, it is responsible for advising the CJCC on integration issues, identifying integration needs, developing integration alternatives, preparing requests for proposals (RFPs), reviewing proposals and making vendor recommendations. Currently, the county/city relationship in the CJCC is based on a memorandum of understanding.

"From a practical standpoint, if this type of intergovernmental endeavor [will] succeed, it is necessary to spell things out in writing," Wiborg said. He added that the MOU has worked thus far, but as the relationships among jurisdictions become more complex, a more detailed document may be necessary to stipulate specific responsibilities and obligations.

Figure 12: The Integrated Systems Advisory Board

Hennepin County Representatives
  Deputy CIO
  IT Specialist (criminal justice)
  County Attorney's Office (2)
  Public Defender's Office (2)
  Sheriff's Office (2)
  Community Corrections Department (3)
City of Minneapolis Representatives
  City Attorney's Office (2)
  Deputy CIO
  Police Department (3)
State of Minnesota Agencies Represented
  Supreme Court
  Department of Public Safety
  Bureau of Criminal Apprehension
  MN Office of Intertechnologies
  Department of Corrections

Fourth Judicial District Representatives
  Court Administrator
  IT Specialist
Hennepin County Suburbs Representatives
  LOGIS
  City of Bloomington Police Department
  City of Brooklyn Park City Attorney
CJCC Representative
  Chair

For more information, contact:

Ron Wiborg, Contracts and Grants Manager

Hennepin County Department of Community Corrections

612–348–7011

E-mail: ron.wiborg@co.hennepin.mn.us

World Wide Web: www.macrogroup.net/cjsiip/project

Scenario

As noted in the Hennepin County case study, Dakota County was the other county in Minnesota that was awarded implementation planning funding in 1999 from the state to develop an integrated justice information system. Dakota will be the first county to test the model being developed by Hennepin County. While this is a new project, working together on technological issues is not new to Dakota County and the cities within the county, which have been participating in the 11-year-old Dakota County geographical information system (GIS) partnership.

The county, along with the cities of Eagan and Burnsville, is the prime mover in the integration effort known as the Criminal Justice Information Integration Network (CJIIN). The initiative to create CJIIN arose out of the monthly meetings of city and county managers and long-running discussions concerning public safety issues. As the lead agency, Dakota County administers the grant.

"The CJIIN is in its infancy," said CJIIN's Project Manager, Mary Cerkvenik, who is also the assistant county administrator of Dakota County. "We have completed the documentation of our current processes; we are almost finished with our current technology model and our data model; and we are now moving into envisioning what we would like our future system to be," Cerkvenik said. "We completed our implementation plan in January 2001." Cerkvenik added that CJIIN started its work on the implementation plan in July 2000. The plan now has been reviewed by CJIIN and its steering committee and currently is being reviewed by state agency representatives.

"All participants are taking great pains to scrutinize their business processes during the planning phases of the integration effort, because those processes must change dramatically before CJIIN is ready to go live," said Kristi Peterson, information technology coordinator of Eagan, Minnesota, and the city's representative on the CJIIN Steering Committee. We knew some of the areas that we were not connecting electronically, but we did not have any idea of how many areas," Peterson said.

Minnesota also selected the three jurisdictions' efforts as a pilot project for the Minnesota Criminal Justice Data Network (CJDN). CJDN will be a private, dedicated network for law enforcement agencies throughout the county that officials hope will ultimately connect more than 400 agencies within the state. Because of this selection, CJDN will provide the primary infrastructure for CJIIN.

"The jurisdictions involved have to move fast," Cerkvenik said. "We are the first county to come in and do an analysis of [the model that Hennepin County created]," she explained. "That is clearly driving our timeline, in that the legislature would like to hear from us for the next legislative session."

Governance Structure

The jurisdictions involved in CJIIN are not working under a memorandum of understanding, as in Hennepin County, or a joint powers agreement (JPA), as is the case in San Diego County, which is discussed later in this chapter.

"Given the culture and the work environment that we found ourselves in, and the relationships that already are established between the different agencies, we are going to get by without having any kind of a formal [document]," said Nancy Harms, assistant administrator of the First Judicial District Court. A management team and a steering committee handle the day-to-day decisions. Spending decisions rest with the County Board of Commissioners. The CJIIN Management Committee consists of 15 members—7 county representatives, 2 representatives each from the cities of Eagan and Burnsville, and 4 representatives from the courts—and meets regularly (see Figure 13). The CJIIN Steering Committee consists of 17 members—9 county representatives, 2 from Eagan, 4 from Burnsville, 1 from the courts, and 1 from the public defender's office (see figure 14).

"When the CJIIN is up and running, a more formal arrangement may be struck between the jurisdictions," said Cerkvenik. "Our city and county managers and the folks on the court side have all been very supportive, have given us some really great staff to work on this project, and have made a commitment to put in the time and effort it takes to make it successful," Cerkvenik said.

"There is no question that there is a lot of good cohesion among us because we have had that support. They have empowered the staff to go forth and do this, and the fact that we do not have a MOU or a JPA is a testament to that."

For more information, contact:

Mary Cerkvenik, Assistant County Administrator
Dakota County
CJIIN Project Manager
651–438–4559
E-mail: Dakota.County.CJIIN@co.dakota.mn.us
World Wide Web:
www.co.dakota.mn.us/sheriff/cjiin/cjiin/htm

Patrice Bataglia, Dakota County Commissioner
651–438–4429
E-mail: patrice.bataglia@co.dakota.mn.us

Figure 13: CJIIN Management Committee

Dakota County representatives
County Administrator
Director of Community Corrections
Sheriff
Director of Community Services
County Attorney
Director of the Office of Management and Budget
Director of Information Technology
Eagan, MN representatives
City Administrator
Police Chief
Courts representatives
First Judicial Administration
Court Administration
Judges
Burnsville, MN representatives
City Manager
Police Chief

Figure 14: CJIIN Steering Committee

Dakota County representatives
Senior Management Analyst, Community Corrections
Manager, Systems & Programming, IT
Assistant County Administrator
Lieutenant, Sheriff's Office
Commander, Sheriff's Office
Chief Deputy; Sheriff's Office First Judicial District Courts
Assistant Judicial Administrator
Chief Public Defender
Assistant County Attorney
County Surveyor
GIS Manager

City of Eagan
IT Coordinator
Captain; Police Department
City of Burnsville
Deputy City Manager
ITC Coordinator
Captain, Police Department
Records Manager, Police Department
Court Representatives
First Judicial District Courts
Assistant Judicial Administrator
Chief Public Defender

Scenario

Marion County was one of the original 10 jurisdictions belonging to the Regional Automated Information Network (RAIN), a justice information network established in 1975. Now, 23 law enforcement agencies from 4 counties, 23 cities, and Western Oregon University are RAIN members. Each member jurisdiction has one vote. RAIN provides a wide range of services to its members, including such systems as

- **Crime Analysis:** a records management incident-reporting system that tracks incident, crime analysis, arrest, missing persons, suspect, victim, vehicle, and property information.
- **Property and Evidence:** a system that records and tracks the movement of property and evidence using bar coding technology.
- **Jail Management:** a system containing booking information, inmates' physical characteristics, court and arresting agency data, inmate charges, time-served data, inmates' aliases, date of birth, and housing information.
- **FILER:** a laptop field-reporting system available to agencies via the Marion/Salem Data Center's FTP (file transfer protocol) Web site.
- **Mugshot Imaging:** a system that includes both adult and juvenile images.
- **Query Management Facility:** a management-reporting function system that includes a large collection of predefined management reports.

In addition, funding has been appropriated to upgrade the FILER system with the addition of a search function for names, incidents, locations, and incident types. At this writing, the upgrade project has not yet started.

Governance Structure

RAIN was created under Oregon Revised Statutes, Chapter 190, which allows separate government entities to create joint, independent organizations. The supervision and management of RAIN are the responsibility of its Policy Board and Executive Committee.

According to the agreement that created RAIN, the policy board:

- Determines the type of services and equipment required to operate RAIN.
- Enters into contracts to acquire goods and services for RAIN.
- Adopts an annual budget for RAIN expenditures and sets the amount of financial participation for each member.
- Creates committees of RAIN members and/or user agency personnel to advise the board.
- Exercises any other power or authority to implement the powers set forth in the agreement that created RAIN.

The RAIN Executive Committee

- Provides advice and assistance to the board.
- Supervises and conducts RAIN's day-to-day operations.
- Conducts regular financial reviews.
- Enters into negotiations or signs contracts on behalf of RAIN, with the proviso that such authority is delegated by the board.

According to Lieutenant Jeff Pikl, staff assistant to RAIN, several user committees answer to the Policy Board and the Executive Committee:

- A user committee comprised of records personnel that coordinates changes, training, and operational issues related to the records-management system.
- A technical committee made up of personnel from video-imaging, field reporting, and evidence/property tracking.
- A futures committee comprised of agency administrators or CEOs that look at trends in technology that might ultimately become enhancements to RAIN's systems.
- A steering committee comprised of the Executive Committee and selected other members for implementing and directing projects such as strategic analysis.

During its long history, RAIN has experienced some growing pains. In the early 1980s, Salem left the RAIN organization and formed the Salem Unified Network (SUN) in partnership with the Marion County/Salem Data Center. During that time, RAIN had its own employees and equipment and provided services directly to its members; but that situation changed in the late 1980s.

In 2000, RAIN and SUN released an RFP for "A Strategic Evaluation and Analysis of the RAIN Consortium and SUN and their RMS Technology Requirements."

"The RFP is looking at where technology is today, whether or not RAIN, in its current form, is still relevant, or should we, again, reconsider the services to members," Robert Tardiff, chief of the Newberg Police Department said. "It is still important to all of us that we share data. At this point, the question is, 'Do we accomplish that by sharing the same programs? Or should RAIN become an organization that provides the mechanism for sharing data from diverse programs, establishes some data standards, and creates some type of process that accomplishes that sharing?"

The RFP, the result of which will cause a change in the way governance is executed, focused on five major areas

1. Defining the purpose of the regional consortia by answering such questions as:
   - Why should RAIN exist?
   - Why should SUN exist?
   - Who should be involved?

Figure 15: RAIN Governance Structure

RAIN Policy Board
One mayor, police chief, city manager or city councilperson, from the 23 cities that participate in RAIN
One sheriff or county commissioner, from the four counties that participate in RAIN

RAIN Executive Committee
Chief of Police, Newberg
Chief of Police, Stayton
Chief of Police, Keizer
Marion County Commissioner
City Manager, Dallas

- Are the geographical boundaries logical?
- Should SUN and RAIN merge?

2. Evaluating the current system.

3. Performing a needs analysis.

4. Proposing alternative methods of providing technology services.

5. Reviewing the current funding streams.

For more information, contact:

Robert Tardiff, Chief of Police
Newberg, Oregon Police Department
Chairman, RAIN Executive Board
503–537–1220
E-mail: tardiff@ci.newberg.or.us

Jeff Pikl, Lieutenant
Stayton, Oregon Police Department
Staff Assistant to RAIN
503–769–3423
E-mail: jpikl@stayton.org
World Wide Web: www.open.org/~rain

SAN DIEGO COUNTY, CALIFORNIA

Scenario

Since the 1970s, San Diego County has participated in the Automated Regional Justice Information System (ARJIS), a project that started as a result of a federal Law Enforcement Assistance Administration award to fund a regional technology system. ARJIS has since grown to comprise more than 35 member agencies and jurisdictions. As Pam Scanlon, the executive director of ARJIS said, "The numbers keep growing."

Ten law enforcement agencies are members of ARJIS—nine police departments and the San Diego County Sheriff's Department. In addition, a blend of state and federal agencies—law enforcement and others, such as the San Diego City Schools and the U.S. Postal Service—are involved with ARJIS as ex officio members.

Today, ARJIS is a multijurisdictional justice information sharing system that contains information on criminal cases, arrests, citations, field interviews, traffic accidents, fraudulent documents, and stolen property. In addition, ARJIS stores regional information on incidents, persons, vehicles, locations, and property. The ARJIS network consists of 659 terminals and printers throughout the county, and ARJIS provides justice information to law enforcement agencies, courts, prosecution, probation departments, corrections departments, juvenile services departments, and the California DMV.

Governance Structure

Created as a joint powers agency, ARJIS is governed by the ARJIS Board of Directors, which involves either mayors or members of city councils from the county's 18 cities and representatives from the county's board of supervisors. Under the board is the Management Committee, which is composed of department heads, such as police chiefs, sheriffs, the county's district attorney and judges. A middle-management group, called the Regional Coordination Committee, is supported by a technical group. A variety of user groups round out the set of governing bodies that keep ARJIS functioning.

ARJIS has a strong governance structure with every agency having one vote. "There's no 800-pound gorilla here, and the Coronados of the world, which have 40 officers, and the San Diego Police Department, which has 2,100 officers—they have the same vote. The police chiefs all treat each other that way too," said Scanlon.

"This has been critical to the success of ARJIS," Scanlon said, noting that the chair positions on the various committees rotate so that each participating jurisdiction in ARJIS has a chance to serve as chair of a committee.

Representatives from the cities of Oceanside and El Cajon told members of the PTI site visit team that the level of equality in ARJIS and the knowledge that their voices will be heard is why they continue to be a part of ARJIS. This contributes to a level of trust that creates a willingness on the part of ARJIS members to make sacrifices when it comes to grant money for which the agencies apply on behalf of ARJIS.

"In the case of the agencies that turn over their grant money for a regional goal, they are not driving the car," Scanlon said. "They are going to get some input, advice, and suggestions from the other agencies and they have to be willing to take those types of recommendations. It is not, 'I'm building this system just for me.'"

One example of the cooperation within ARJIS is the ARJIS Web site's regional mapping application, which was created through a $70,000 grant to the San Diego Police Department (SDPD). SDPD turned grant funds over to ARJIS, which matched the dollar figure, leaving ARJIS $140,000 to invest in developing the regional mapping application. The department, because it contributed such a large chunk of money, was closely involved with the project, but the application still had to win ultimate approval from the ARJIS Board of Directors. The project won the 2000 Helen Putnam Award for Excellence from the California League of Cities.

Some of the agencies hesitated when we first talked about the mapping application," Scanlon said. "But through collective reasoning, they were able to see the benefit. We do have doubters, and we have got agencies that question it. It is not a bed of roses. But there is a tremendous environment of trust built up. I also believe that we are demonstrating success. We are turning out products, and we are very open in our iterative process of product development."

In the end, "A strong governance structure is what makes ARJIS tick," Scanlon said. "Some agencies don't believe you need a governance structure," she said. "It is the chicken and the egg argument: 'Do you get your system or money first, or do you start your governance structure first?' It does not have to be, 'Oh, we have $15 million, how do we spend it?' There's a whole bunch of issues that governance boards can look at."

For more information, contact:

Pam Scanlon, Executive Director, ARJIS
858–581–9717
E-mail: plb@dpc.sannet.gov
World Wide Web: www.ARJIS.org

Scenario

Henrico County currently does not operate an integrated justice information system. However, the county's actions do offer lessons for those jurisdictions in the prejustice integration phase that are pursuing a course of action that could lead to an integrated justice information system.

For the last year, the county has used an 800 MHz radio system that handles the needs of all its departments, especially public safety agencies. Chesterfield County and Richmond approached the same vendor used by Henrico County with the ultimate goal of implementing radio systems identical to that of Henrico County. When that happens, each jurisdiction will operate its system independently and have its own communications center, but the three systems will be interoperable.

At that point, a Henrico County law enforcement officer will be able to travel between the jurisdictions and communicate not only with the home communications center, but also with law enforcement agencies from Chesterfield County and Richmond. Richmond and Henrico and Chesterfield Counties are not sharing data automatically through integrated systems, although Henrico County's law enforcement personnel can query wanted/warrant files, but only for Richmond. Henrico County has a mobile-data system and is encouraging Richmond and Chesterfield County to obtain such a system so that all three jurisdictions can share information.

Governance Structure

While integration efforts are in their infancy, the need to address governance has been identified. The chief administrative officers from Richmond and Henrico and Chesterfield Counties created a steering committee 3 years ago to orchestrate the integration effort. The steering committee reviews projects, prioritizes initiatives and sets policy and standards. It also has formed policies regarding data ownership. Subcommittees handle matters related to the implementation of the radio systems, coordinating operational protocols, etc.

The steering committee was created by the signing of a Capital Region Communications Memorandum of Understanding (see figure 16). This MOU was signed approximately 3 years ago and stipulates that the chief administrators of each locality are to appoint representatives who will be responsible for the initiation of this cooperative effort. Further, they will be responsible for continuing operations affected by mutually agreed-to resource sharing and establishment of those policies and procedures which may be necessary to ensure continued cooperation and consistent operational capabilities for all public-safety systems.

Henrico County's manager played an essential role in creating the MOU among the jurisdictions. While the MOU is the document that created the steering committee, its language is not particularly specific. Participation is voluntary, and there is no set term for participation for members of either the steering committee or the subcommittees. The governing body created by Henrico County is a forum that unites participants in working toward the shared goals of improving communication among agencies and improving the ability of staff to do their jobs.

"We believe that the most important ingredient of any multijurisdictional project, especially in the field of public safety communications, is a mechanism that will enhance the sharing of open and honest communications among the participants," said Paul Proto, chairman of the steering committee and Henrico County's Director of General Services.

For more information, contact:
Paul Proto, Director of General Services
Henrico County
Chairman of the Steering Committee
804–501–4957
E-mail: pro@co.henrico.va.us

TILLAMOOK COUNTY, OREGON

Scenario

Justice information integration is currently limited to the county's law enforcement agencies receiving information from state-operated systems, such as the State Patrol. This is a common occurrence at the beginning stages of a broader effort. However, the county is pursuing several initiatives, which are expected to evolve into a justice information integration system.

The county is one of six in Oregon that received grant money from the federal Office of Juvenile Justice and Delinquency Prevention to perform data gathering and information sharing in the juvenile justice field. Furthermore, in 1999, the Oregon Legislature passed legislation targeted at juvenile crime prevention, with the state disbursing grant money to each county for crime prevention and basic services. Particularly, the legislation helped create a uniform assessment for county juvenile departments to help streamline data gathering.

The legislation requires all counties in the state to create a coordinated juvenile justice plan that focuses on 10- to 18-year-old offenders. Oregon law requires this plan to provide coordination of communitywide services, including prevention, treatment, education, employment resources, and intervention strategies.

Governance Structure

Established legislation requires counties to create a Local Public Safety Coordinating Council (LPSCC) for coordinating criminal justice policy among agencies and juvenile-justice agencies (see figure 17). The county sheriff is the chair of the council, and participating agencies include community corrections, a county commissioner, a local district attorney, representatives from the county's Juvenile Department, and representatives from the county's Commission on Children and Families.

As its roster indicates, the LPSCC is made up of the key members of the agencies involved—an essential element crucial to the success of any governing body that jurisdictions or agencies create to oversee integration efforts. Among its many responsibilities,

PROFILE

This rural county is located on the Pacific coast near the Washington/Oregon border and covers 1,125 square miles. U.S. Census Bureau estimates for 1999 put the county's population at approximately 24,420. Like other small, rural counties, Tillamook has a low population density and is home to a small number of sparsely populated cities—seven, in fact, which are Bay City, Garibaldi, Manzanita, Nehalem, Rockaway Beach, Tillamook, and Wheeler.

Figure 17: Composition of the LPSCC

A police chief
The sheriff of the county
The county's district attorney
A state court judge
A public defender or defense attorney
A director of community corrections
A county commissioner
A juvenile department director
A director of the county's health departments
A member of the general public
A representative of the Oregon State Police
A representative of the Oregon Youth Authority
A city council person or mayor and a city manager
   or other city representative

LPSCC must create and recommend a plan—to individual county boards of commissioners—that uses state and local resources to serve both the needs of adult criminal offenders in the county and of those offenders 10 to 18 years of age. For the eventual pursuit of justice information systems integration, the statute requires LPSCC to coordinate local criminal justice policy among affected criminal justice entities.

Because representatives from various justice agencies already work together, LPSCC's governance structure offers another organizational model for creating a governance structure dedicated to overseeing integration efforts.

"The strength of the LPSCC is getting all the decisionmakers together in one place," former County Commissioner Gina Firman said. "It makes it much easier to talk about the plans that are required to get federal grants, to get state grants—to do almost anything, if you have to have a plan that's been signed off on. Before, what was happening was that one person would have to run this plan around to all of the different agencies. Now we are meeting at least on a quarterly basis and sometimes more frequently, depending on what planning processes we are going through."

Although state law created the county's LPSCC, other jurisdictions should have the ability to easily create similar governance structures. Firman recommended, for example, that groups devise a simple mission statement, but specify membership requirements.

The county's law enforcement agencies have worked long and hard to develop a culture that supports cooperation and honesty among agencies, and Tillamook County logically benefits from the rapport of an intimate law enforcement community. "The police chiefs in the county's towns and the sheriff have gotten together informally once a month for coffee down at the local restaurant," Firman said. "That is where the law enforcement piece already had a history. What has been added to that are the other sides of law enforcement—the Commission on Children and Families, the juvenile justice department, community corrections, attorneys, and judges."

In a rural jurisdiction like Tillamook, information requests are processed rapidly between law enforcement agencies because of the tight-knit community. "If they call each other for help or information, there's a fairly strong inclination to cooperate because they're going to see each other at the little league game that night," said Firman. "You can't treat somebody poorly on the phone during the day and then go sit next to them in the bleachers that night. There seems to be a good mesh of personalities that work well together."

For more information, contact:
Gina Firman, former County Commissioner
Tillamook County
503–399–7201
E-mail: gfirman@orlocalgov.org
Dan Krein, Director, Juvenile Department
Tillamook County
E-mail: DKREIN@co.tillamook.or.us

Chapter 8
Recommendations

Recommendations for Establishing Local Governance Structures

When survey participants were asked to list three top recommendations for establishing local governance structures that can facilitate the integration of justice information systems, their responses coalesced around five themes:

1. Ensure equal involvement/participation from all agencies/jurisdictions involved.

2. Explore and secure funding.

3. Set realistic goals and objectives with a reasonable timeframe for the plan—prepare a mission statement.

4. Keep on-going, open lines of communications with all agencies/ jurisdictions involved.

5. Have unconditional support of county boards/city councils/elected officials.

1. Ensure equal involvement/participation from all agencies/jurisdictions involved

Throughout the survey, participants mentioned turf battles as an impediment to the integration of the necessary systems. These can take many forms, including which jurisdiction or agency has ownership of the data and the power to control access to it. Turf battles can be significantly reduced or eliminated if all relevant agencies/jurisdictions are brought to the table and allowed equal involvement and participation. Justice information system integration needs to stretch beyond jurisdictional boundaries; therefore, the list of agencies that must be involved should not be restricted to one jurisdiction's boundaries. The San Diego case study presented in the previous chapter demonstrates the kind of success that can be achieved when there is equal representation and participation among all agencies involved.

2. Explore and secure funding

Funding problems and concerns were consistently expressed throughout the survey. Funding or lack of funding was suggested as a major reason why jurisdictions were not involved in justice integration. Those involved in integration saw funding as a consistent problem in their implementation of integration. Respondents remarked about the high cost of not only implementing integration, but maintaining and upgrading their systems as well. The success or failure of integration can be, and often is, directly related to funding issues.

3. Set realistic goals and objectives with a reasonable timeframe for the plan— prepare a mission statement

Most of the jurisdictions did not have operational plans for the integration of their systems. Some had not set goals while others had set goals that could not be achieved, often based on factors beyond their control. The adoption of an operational plan and mission statement early in the process may make the difference between success or failure. In planning, immediate short-term successes that can be achieved early in the integration process should be identified. These early victories will motivate participants to strive for bigger, longer-term accomplishments.

4. Keep ongoing, open lines of communications with all agencies/ jurisdictions involved

A governance structure helps to facilitate ongoing dialog and other communication between the various parties involved in the integration. In the creation of a structure, all affected parties should be brought to the table. Once there, all participants should be open and honest about their needs and concerns. Structures can be destroyed when decisions are made by cliques within the structure, when essential parties are excluded from the communication links, and when parties involved are not open and honest.

5. Have unconditional support of county boards/city councils/elected officials

Many efforts have failed because they did not have the support of the elected officials. When the officials were needed to provide funding, statutory authority or some other decisionmaking outcome, many officials have made the wrong decisions because of ignorance of the project. Others have been slow to sign on because they were not included in the planning process. Good leadership was mentioned by respondents with successful integration projects as critical to their success. Sometimes that leadership came from elected officials.

Obstacles To Be Avoided in Implementing an Integrated Justice System Governance Structure

When queried to list major obstacles jurisdictions should try to avoid in developing and/or implementing an integrated justice governance structure, four central themes were identified:

1. Turf issues of users, agencies, or governmental bodies.
2. Politics.
3. Inadequate funding.
4. Technology (lack of field testing of hardware or software, inadequate equipment, and untrained personnel and support staff).

Integration Recommendations to Justice Agencies

The three main recommendations that survey participants would make to justice agencies with respect to the integration of information systems related to:

1. Technology (train in-house users and support staff; standardize and network all software, hardware and protocols; and utilize up-to-date equipment).
2. Security of information and security measures.
3. Identification and agreement on information to be shared and standardize forms for entry of information.

1. Technology

There are numerous issues related to technology that need to be of concern to criminal justice professionals who are engaged in information integration. Some jurisdictions have as many as five information systems that do not communicate with each other, and no one on staff can fix the problem or the problem cannot be fixed with existing software. Some jurisdictions have wasted money on unnecessary or underutilized technology sold to them by consultants or vendors. Lacking the staff to implement integration, operation, and maintenance of these systems, expensive hardware and software will not solve integration problems. Conversely, other jurisdictions have poured money into outdated equipment that does not have the capability to carry out varied functions and cannot be updated to meet emerging situations.

2. Security of information and security measures

Concerns about the security of justice information has been a primary factor in preventing justice information systems integration. Law enforcement officials often do not trust other elements of the system to network with their systems for fear of compromising their data security. This is a valid concern, but it is not an insurmountable one. The incorporation of appropriate security measures and firewalls can protect the integrity of integrated systems.

3. Identification and agreement on information sharing

In the planning process, the agencies/jurisdictions involved should collectively select the types and nature of information to be shared and the forms that will be used for data entry. A governance structure is the appropriate mechanism to facilitate the selection of data to be shared and forms to be used.

Integration Obstacles To Avoid

There were four major obstacles to the integration of justice information systems identified. These obstacles are very similar to the obstacles to avoid when developing and implementing a governance structure, as listed above.

1. Turf wars and politics.
2. Lack of standardized equipment (software and hardware), lack of networking among agencies, and use of old technology.
3. Lack of funding for implementation and future expansion of systems.
4. Lack of concrete plan with commitment from all agencies.

The presence or lack of technology remains a crucial factor in the success of an integration effort, yet it does not guarantee the occurrence of integration. By itself, technology cannot solve all system integration problems and even the best-equipped integration effort will bog down without an effective governing body charting the path. Any project's path will be littered with pitfalls and false trails. However, the integration of justice information systems creates its own unique problems. Time and again, survey respondents asserted that a governing body with committed leadership, that orchestrates a well-conceived plan and is built on equal participation by those agencies or jurisdictions involved is the best way to solve inherent problems.

Unsurprisingly, respondents rated turf issues high on the list of barriers to creating effective governance structures. That same issue also was identified in a completely separate research project conducted by the Center for Technology in Government, State University of New York at Albany. According to the center's study, the concept of turf generally included at least three major reasons organizations act defensively:

1. To avoid the costs of change.

2. To reduce or control risk.

3. To preserve autonomy or protect their position in a competitive or adversarial environment.

Integration typically requires a degree of centralized control and shared decisionmaking that could decrease an agency's control of its operations or resources. Protecting turf can be particularly important when the potential loss of autonomy or control could benefit other agencies that are political or institutional competitors.

The governance structure, in its different forms, provides the foundation for an environment of trust and communication. During PTI's site visits, several of the jurisdictions indicated that their integration efforts started years ago through informal discussions of city managers or county supervisors or through information system users at agencies who, during casual discussion, saw a way to perform their jobs better.

Building a Governance Structure

Perhaps the most important item to keep in mind is that governance structures can be formal or informal. Also, governance structures can be created in a number of ways: through state law, through memoranda of understanding signed by agencies within a jurisdiction, through a joint powers agreement signed by agencies in separate jurisdictions or by several jurisdictions in a region, or through signed charters or other agreements. Whatever the vehicle, the document should be a statement of general goals that identifies the members and the decisionmaking process.

The document for creating the overall governance structure should identify committee participants and note their commitment so that key players attend meetings. This helps to avoid the potential problem of executive officers from the representative agencies or jurisdictions lacking the commitment to devote time and energy to the governance structure.

Respondents from jurisdictions that are not currently engaged in justice integration efforts and that do not have a governance structure to oversee integration identified the lack of funding as the number one barrier to their integration efforts. Those respondents said that funding was a primary resource that federal, state, and regional entities could make available to assist them in initiating a justice information integration project. If funding is an issue for a jurisdiction, the governing body can solicit assistance from a dedicated funding source.

Besides identifying and applying for funding, the committees and governing boards created by a governance structure help move the business of integrating justice information systems forward. Another important aspect to creating the governance structure is the level of jurisdictional and agency equality the structure brings to the integration effort. Besides setting direction, a governance structure also can set the stage for involvement by small agencies that might not otherwise have the resources or the inclination to participate in a large agency dominated regional consortium.

Implementing a Structure

Once the structure is established, the work begins. The next challenge is to ensure that the work does not bog down and that all participating agencies are making progress toward achieving system integration goals. Maintaining enthusiasm is critical; something as seemingly minor as what day to schedule the monthly meetings can slow the workflow. While the timing of meetings is important, the governance structure must also ensure that the right level of personnel makes up the committees that handle the day-to-day work of the justice integration effort. Presenting the right kind of information to the right committee also is crucial.

Maintaining the Structure

While the original document creating the governance structure may meet the needs of the participating cities or counties and agencies, it may require revision as the integration of justice information systems continues. Through the survey and site visits, PTI found that maintaining the governance structure and the integration effort entails a different set of needs than creating either of them. Periodically revisiting the document that created the structure helps cities, counties, and participating agencies ensure that the document is still valid.

Governance structures must also weather political storms. Because elected officials typically hold seats on committees or governing boards, the governance structure is affected by the political cycles. The composition of the structure may change radically every 2 or 4 years, and it is possible to lose a strong supporter to the winds of political change. However, this does not overshadow the important contributions that elected officials can make to the governance structures overseeing justice integration efforts. In addition, political change affects key appointed officials, such as city and county managers.

Both elected and appointed officials play vital roles in the development, implementation, and institutionalization processes. Elected officials, for example, can give governance structures a voice in the political arena, can give structures statutory authority, and can help to fund integration projects. Appointed officials, on the other hand, can bring professional management techniques to the process.

The survey revealed the need for the integration effort to have a champion. In times of political turnover, the project's champion can work with newly elected officials to help them understand the benefits of integration and the value in maintaining their jurisdiction's or agency's commitment to the integration effort through to its successful conclusion. Such a champion can keep the structure functioning while the new players are learning the process.

Postscript

The momentum for integrating justice information systems is building across the country, and as the survey and case studies have demonstrated, justice agencies and jurisdictions are dedicating significant resources and personnel time to interoperability. Soon, systems will exist that transport information across jurisdictional and institutional lines, making that information available in real time to those who need it when they need it. The passion for this vision is hard at work.

The conclusions reached by the survey and site visits complement the findings of the Conference of States and other sessions held in 1997–98 (see chapter 2, The Role of the Federal Government) that a governance structure is essential to any successful effort to integrate local (and state) justice information systems. Information contained in this guidebook should be shared with others. Integrated systems are essential to the future of processes that provide efficient, fair and timely justice. Elected leaders, key managers of agencies involved in the criminal justice system, as well as the public at large, must be educated on the need and agency capacity for constructing an integrated justice information system and the governance structure that supports it. Jurisdictions presently engaged in integration must actively share their experiences so that others can benefit from their successes and learn from their failures.

Upon completion of its task, the working group felt strongly that this guidebook should be used as a proactive tool for education and outreach to jurisdictions nationwide. A key result of the survey and site visit findings identified the need for buy-in and committed support of local elected and appointed officials for any integrated justice effort to be successful. However, there is a need to enhance the knowledge and understanding of the often complex issues involved for local leaders. The group felt that this guidebook (and survey) also should be updated regularly to maintain the database of knowledge on the progress being made within and among local governments and their state and federal counterparts. This will enable the U.S. Department of Justice to monitor progress in a broad range of areas, including whether or not state and federal assistance is helping, and to target limited resources. Jurisdictions then can be tracked using the data collected. The group also felt that training at the "101" level is critical in integrated systems and that it benefits governance structure building, especially regarding strategic planning, funding issues, growing professional staff, and procurement issues.

Although integration may not yet enjoy popular support, it offers a key ingredient to the success of justice systems, and the governance of integrated justice systems offers a key ingredient for effective operation.

Appendix A
Survey Instrument

Local Governance Survey
Section I
Respondent Profile

Name:_____Title: _____

Jurisdiction: _____

Mailing Address (please provide street address rather than P.O. Box)

_____

_____

Phone: _____ Fax:_____ E-mail: _____

1. **Check all of the applicable attributes that primarily apply to your jurisdiction.**

    a. ❐ Rural   ❐ Urban   ❐ Suburban

    b. ❐ Population less than 10,000   ❐ 10,000–50,000   ❐ 50,000–100,000   ❐ 100,000–250,000   ❐ Over 250,000

    c. ❐ City   ❐ County   ❐ City/County

2. **What form of government applies to your jurisdiction?**

    ❐ Mayor/Council   ❐ Council/Manager   ❐ County Executive/Commission   ❐ County Manager/Commission

    ❐ Other_____

3. **What local government agency or department do you represent?**

    _____

    If you are the Information Technology (IT) Department is it jurisdictionwide or department within a specific agency?

    ❐ Jurisdictionwide   ❐ Department within a specific agency

4. **Do your job responsibilities involve sharing information/data input and output with other departments, agencies, jurisdictions and/or the state?**   ❐ Yes   ❐ No

    If No: Who in your department/agency does (position/title)? _____

5. **Does your agency operate information systems that are integrated with systems of other departments/agencies?**
    ❐ Yes   ❐ No
    If yes, with which of the following department(s)/agency(s) is your system integrated? (Check all that apply)
    Criminal Justice/Public Safety Agencies

❐ Law enforcement	❐ Court	❐ Corrections	❐ Probation
❐ Public Defender	❐ Juvenile Services	❐ Department of Motor Vehicles	❐ Fire
❐ Emergency Communications	❐ Emergency Medical	❐ Parole	
❐ Prosecution	❐ Other: _____		

    Non-Criminal Justice/Non-Public Safety Agencies

❐ Child Support Agency	❐ Social Service	❐ Health Department	❐ Education
❐ Public Utilities	❐ Planning/Zoning	❐ Transportation	
❐ Victim Support Groups	❐ Public Works		
❐ Other:_____			

If you selected any of the above agency categories, please identify the agency/department and the type of information they access.

a. Agency_____ Information Accessed_____

b. Agency_____ Information Accessed_____

c. Agency_____ Information Accessed_____

6. Does your jurisdiction operate information systems that are integrated with systems of other local jurisdictions?

❏ Yes   ❏ No

If yes, please identify the departments. (Check all that apply)

Criminal Justice/Public Safety Agencies

❏ Law Enforcement	❏ Court	❏ Corrections	❏ Probation
❏ Public Defender	❏ Juvenile Services	❏ Department of Motor Vehicles	❏ Fire
❏ Emergency Communications	❏ Emergency Medical	❏ Parole	
❏ Prosecution	❏ Other: _____		

Non-Criminal Justice/Non-Public Safety Agencies

❏ Child Support Agency	❏ Social Service	❏ Health Department	❏ Education
❏ Public Utilities	❏ Planning/Zoning	❏ Transportation	
❏ Victim Support Groups	❏ Public Works		

❏ Other:_____

If you selected any of the above agency categories, please identify the agency/department and the type of information they access.

a. Agency_____ Information Accessed_____

b. Agency_____ Information Accessed_____

c. Agency_____ Information Accessed_____

7. Does your jurisdiction operate information systems that are integrated with state criminal justice information systems?   ❏ Yes   ❏ No

8. Has your jurisdiction implemented public access rules or structures for accessing data? ❏ Yes   ❏ No

9. Has your jurisdiction developed an integrated information technology strategic plan?   ❏ Yes   ❏ No

If yes, would you provide a copy upon request?   ❏ Yes   ❏ No

10. Which of the following best describes the status of your jurisdiction's criminal justice/public safety integration efforts and the governance structure to facilitate such integration?

A. ❏ We have no criminal justice/public safety integration effort underway nor a governance structure to facilitate such integration. (Proceed to section II)

B. ❏ We have a governance structure to facilitate the integration of our criminal justice/public safety information systems but are currently not integrating our criminal justice/public safety information systems. (Skip to section III)

C. ❏ We are integrating our criminal justice/public safety information systems but have not put in place a governance structure. (Skip to section IV)

D. ❏ We are integrating our criminal justice/public safety information systems and have in place a governance structure to facilitate such integration. (Skip to section III)

Section II
No Integration/No Governance Structure

(Response A to Question 10)

11. Please check all appropriate reasons why your jurisdiction is not engaged in the integration of its criminal justice/public safety information systems.

- ❐ Politics
- ❐ Size of Relevant Agency(ies)
- ❐ Trust
- ❐ Risk Management/Exposure
- ❐ Power/control
- ❐ Liability
- ❐ Agency "Cultural" Issues
- ❐ Data/Information Security
- ❐ Funding
- ❐ Other: _____

12. Has your jurisdiction attempted to establish a governance structure to facilitate the integration of a criminal justice/public safety information system in the past?

- ❐ Yes
- ❐ No

If yes, please describe the effort and the major reasons that it was not successful. _____

_____

13. What are the primary reasons that your jurisdiction has not established a governance structure to facilitate the integration of its criminal justice/public safety information systems?

- ❐ Politics
- ❐ Size of relevant agency(ies)
- ❐ Trust
- ❐ Risk Management/Exposure
- ❐ Power/Control
- ❐ Liability
- ❐ Agency "Cultural" Issue
- ❐ Data/Information Security
- ❐ Funding
- ❐ Other: _____

14. Has your jurisdiction made attempts to integrate its criminal justice/public safety information system in the past?   ❐ Yes   ❐ No

If yes, please describe the effort and the major reason(s) why it was not successful._____

_____

15. If your jurisdiction were to integrate its criminal justice/public safety agency(ies) information system, which of the following would most likely be included? (Check all that apply)

- ❐ Law Enforcement
- ❐ Courts
- ❐ Corrections
- ❐ Probation
- ❐ Parole
- ❐ Prosecutor
- ❐ Public Defender
- ❐ Schools
- ❐ Juvenile Justice
- ❐ Fire
- ❐ EMS
- ❐ Transportation
- ❐ Emergency Communications
- ❐ Department of Motor Vehicles
- ❐ Social Services
- ❐ Health Department
- ❐ Other: _____

16. Which of the following are the barriers to integrating your jurisdiction's criminal justice/public safety information system? (Please check all that apply and explain why you consider this a barrier in the space provided)

- ❐ Funding
- ❐ Turf Issues
- ❐ Liability
- ❐ Lack of Champion
- ❐ Size of Agency(ies)
- ❐ Agency "Cultural" Issues
- ❐ Political
- ❐ Liability
- ❐ Trust
- ❐ Lack of Governance Structure
- ❐ Liability
- ❐ Technology Issues
- ❐ Staffing/Personnel
- ❐ Liability
- ❐ Risk Management/Exposure
- ❐ Other:_____
- ❐ Other:_____

17. **What outside assistance would help your jurisdiction engage in the integration of its criminal justice/public safety information system(s)? (Identify all that apply by distinguishing whether it is Federal (F), State (S), Regional (R), or Local (L)) You may choose more than one level.**

Federal (F)	State (S)	Regional (R)	Local (L)

Funding   Industry

Strategic Planning   Staff/Personnel

Implementation   Marketing Plan

Facilitation Operation & Management   Plans/Budgeting

Consultants   Public/Private Partnership

❐ Other:_____   ❐ Other:_____

18. **Does your state have a statewide information integration planning effort underway?**

❐ Yes   ❐ No   ❐ Don't Know

If yes, how did you learn of the effort? (Please check all that apply)

❐ Your jurisdiction was notified.   ❐ Your agency was notified.

❐ Your jurisdiction was invited to the table. ❐ Your agency was invited to the table.

❐ Read about it.   ❐ Other: _____

If yes, is your jurisdiction participating in this effort?   ❐ Yes   ❐ No

If yes, is your jurisdiction required to adhere to any established guidelines?   ❐ Yes   ❐ No

If yes, would a copy of those guidelines be available upon request?   ❐ Yes   ❐ No

Please skip to section V to complete the survey.

Section III
No Integration/Have Government Structure(s)

Your jurisdiction has a governance structure but may or may not be engaged in integrating its criminal justice/public safety information system(s).

"Yes" Governance Structure—"No" Integration (Answer B to Question 10)   Or

"Yes" Governance Structure—"Yes" Integration (Answer D to Question 10)

19. **Which of the following best describes your jurisdiction's governance structure:**

❐ A group created by statute or ordinance.

❐ A group established as a requirement for receiving a grant.

❐ A group of criminal justice/public safety agency/department representatives was formed through a cooperative agreement, memorandum of understanding, etc.

❐ A loose configuration with informal guidelines.

❐ A group created for a broader purpose than integrated criminal justice/public safety systems.

❐ A single individual/agency responsible for the jurisdiction's IT department.

❐ Our jurisdiction has multiple governance structures.

❐ Other: _____

20. Which of the following best describes how the governance structure was initiated?

❏ Originally created for another purpose.

❏ Created because of a legislated mandate.

❏ Initiated by affected agency personnel.

❏ Advocated for and formed by a key advocate/champion.

❏ Other: _____

If you selected key advocate/champion, please explain who or what entity was the driving force?_____

21. Which of the following agencies/individuals participate in the governance structure? (Please check all that apply)

❏ Law enforcement   ❏ Courts   ❏ Central IT Agency   ❏ Corrections

❏ Prosecutor ❏ Parole   ❏ Chief Elected Official   ❏ Probation

❏ Criminal Defense   ❏ Chief Appointed Official   ❏ State Criminal Justice/Public Safety Agency(ies)

❏ Other:_____   ❏ Other:_____

If State Criminal Justice/Public Safety Agencies: Please name them_____

_____

22. How are the governance body members selected?

❏ Vote   ❏ Study   ❏ Resolution   ❏ Appointment

❏ Other:_____

23. Has your jurisdiction's governance body established rules, policies or statutes that establish ownership of data?

❏ Yes   ❏ No

24. Does the governance structure have fiscal authority?

❏ Yes   ❏ No

If yes, does it have   ❏ taxing authority   ❏ no taxing authority   ❏ spending authority

25. What are the roles/responsibilities of the governance board? (Check all that apply)

❏ Review projects   ❏ Recommend funding   ❏ Approve funding

❏ Prioritize initiatives   ❏ Set standards   ❏ Prioritize system changes

❏ Set policy   ❏ Authorize software programming

❏ Oversee daily operations   ❏ Other: _____

❏ Other:_____   ❏ Other:_____

26. Within your jurisdiction who (position/title) and what agency makes the following policy recommendations for the operation and maintenance of your information system(s).

Policy Recommendation	Position/Title	Agency
❏ Access to database		
❏ Release of information		
❏ Development of new services		
❏ Upgrades for system		
❏ Funding		
❏ Staffing/personnel		

27. Does the governance body have its own staff?　　　　❏ Yes　　　　❏ No

28. To whom or what entity does the governance body report?

❏ City Council　　　　❏ County Commission　　　　❏ City Manager

❏ County Manager　　　❏ Mayor　　　　　　　　　　❏ County Executive

❏ User Agencies　　　　❏ Regional Authority　　　　❏ Other: _____

29. How is the success of the governance board measured?

❏ Proper expenditure of funds　　❏ Successful integration　　❏ Speed of decisionmaking

❏ Proper vendor selection　　　　❏ Integration/activation in a timely manner

❏ Enhancing crime solving　　　　❏ Meets needs of member agencies

❏ Other: _____

30. How much involvement has your jurisdiction's criminal justice/public safety governance body had in the federal justice integration effort?

❏ Your agency/jurisdiction has received a federal grant(s)

❏ Your agency/jurisdiction is contemplating applying for a federal grant(s)

❏ Your jurisdiction is actively involved in NCIC 2000 or III changes

❏ You are unaware of federal efforts

❏ Other: _____

31. What three factors have had a positive impact on your jurisdiction's governance structure?

1. _____

2. _____

3. _____

Why have these factors had a positive impact on your jurisdiction's governance structure?

_____

_____

32. What three factors have had a negative impact on your jurisdiction's governance structure?

1. _____

2. _____

3. _____

Why have these factors had a negative impact on your jurisdiction's governance?

_____

_____

_____

33. How is the governance body funded? Check all that apply

❏ Federal block grant(s)　　❏ Private funding　　❏ State funding　　❏ Capital improvement project

❏ Normal operating budget　❏ Not funded　　　　❏ Not sure　　　　❏ Other:_____

34. Does your jurisdiction have any unique/innovative mechanisms for funding the governance structure?
If yes, briefly explain. _____

_____

35. How have changes in your jurisdiction's overall funding priorities effected funding stream(s) for the governance body? Explain briefly. _____

_____

_____

36. How much involvement has your local governance body had in the statewide criminal justice/public safety integration effort?

❏ State has mandated participation.   ❏ You are unaware of any state integration effort.

❏ Your jurisdiction has been invited to participate voluntarily.   ❏ Your agency/jurisdiction has received a state grant.

❏ You are aware of state efforts but have not participated.   ❏ Other: _____

37. How are your jurisdiction's local elected officials involved in the governance structure?

❏ The governance structure is mandated by local elected officials.

❏ The governance structure is funded by local elected officials.

❏ The jurisdiction's local elected officials are not aware of the governance structure.

❏ Elected officials participate in the governance structure.

❏ Other: _____

38. Do all participants in the governance structure have an equal voice in the decisionmaking process?

❏ Yes   ❏ No

If no, which agencies or individuals (titles) hold decisionmaking authority?

_____

**If you have NO criminal justice/public safety integration underway,
(and answered question 10 with a B) please skip to section V.**

**If you HAVE a criminal justice/public safety integration effort underway,
(and answered question 10 with a D) please continue with section IV.**

Section IV
Have Integration Effort, May or May Not Have Governance Structure

Have a Criminal Justice/Public Safety Integration Effort but May or May Not Have a Governance Structure

Yes Integration—No Governance (Response C to Question 10) or

Yes Integration—Yes Governance (Response D to Question 10)

39. **What type of criminal justice/public safety information system(s) integration is your jurisdiction involved in?**
    (Check all that apply)

    ❏ Within a single agency   ❏ Between agencies of jurisdictions across state boundary

    ❏ Between agencies within the jurisdiction   ❏ Between agencies of outside Jurisdiction(s) or regionally

    ❏ Other: _____

40. **How did your jurisdiction's criminal justice/public safety integration process start?**

    ❏ Between agencies of outside jurisdiction(s) or regionally

    ❏ Grass roots effort   ❏ Mandate by statute   ❏ Initiated by top staff

    ❏ Federal/state grant   ❏ Interlocal agreement   ❏ Advisory group/association

    ❏ Other: _____

41. **If your jurisdiction is involved in a multijurisdictional integration effort, how many of each of the following city**
    or county agencies is involved? (Put number in blank by agency's name)

    ❏ Law Enforcement   ❏ Courts   ❏ Corrections   ❏ Parole

    ❏ Probation   ❏ Prosecutor   ❏ Public Defender   ❏ Other:_____

42. **Which of the following state agencies is involved? (Check all that apply)**

    ❏ Office of Public Safety/State Police   ❏ Bureau of Criminal Investigation   ❏ Corrections

    ❏ Bureau of Criminal Identification   ❏ Attorney General's Office   ❏ Parole

    ❏ Courts   ❏ Probation   ❏ Pretrial Detention

    ❏ Prosecutor   ❏ Juvenile Services   ❏ Public Defender

    ❏ Chief Information Officer   ❏ Criminal Justice Planning   ❏ Department of Motor Vehicles

    ❏ Child Welfare/Protection   ❏ Mental Health   ❏ Health and Social Services

    ❏ None

43. **Is your jurisdiction's criminal justice/public safety information system(s) integrating with private or media**
    groups?   ❏ Yes   ❏ No

44. **How does your jurisdiction's integration process operate?**

    ❏ Single point of entry   ❏ Reentry of data into shared access systems

    ❏ Bidirectional data flow   ❏ One-way data flow   ❏ Other: _____

45. **Are there any rules, policies or statutes that establish ownership of data?**   ❏ Yes   ❏ No

46. **Please identify all agencies within your jurisdiction that are involved in its integration effort.**
    (Check all that apply)

    ❏ Law Enforcement   ❏ Courts   ❏ Corrections   ❏ Probation   ❏ Parole   ❏ Prosecution

    ❏ Public Defender   Other:_____

47. Please identify all agencies of outside jurisdictions that are involved in your jurisdiction's integration effort. (Check all that apply)

❒ Law Enforcement   ❒ Courts   ❒ Corrections   ❒ Probation   ❒ Parole   ❒ Prosecution

❒ Public Defender   ❒ Other:_____   Other:_____

48. Which of the following standards is in place?

❒ Data standards   ❒ Open systems   ❒ Network   ❒ Protocol   ❒ Security

❒ Other:_____

49. If your agency's system(s) are integrated with other data/information systems, please identify those that apply.

❒ Offender-based Tracking/Transaction System   ❒ Computer-aided Dispatch (CAD)   ❒ Records Management System

❒ Offender History   ❒ Juvenile Data   ❒ Case Management

❒ Fingerprint System   ❒ Geographic Information Systems   ❒ Fire/Arson

❒ Court Dispositions   ❒ Corrections   ❒ Gun Dealers

❒ Other: _____

50. What mandates, if any apply for data sharing? (Check all that apply)

❒ State Statute   ❒ Local Ordinance   ❒ Jurisdictional Policy

❒ Mutual Agreements   ❒ Professional Practice   ❒ None

❒ Other: _____

51. What barriers to integration has your jurisdiction faced? (Check all that apply)

❒ Funding   ❒ Lack of Support   ❒ Lack of Governance Structure

❒ Political Issues   ❒ Turf Issues   ❒ Staffing/Personnel

❒ Lack of Strategic Planning   ❒ Technology Issues   ❒ Other: _____

52. Would/does a governance structure benefit your jurisdiction's integration efforts?   ❒ Yes   ❒ No

If yes, what would be (are) the benefit(s)?

_____

_____

If no, why not? _____

_____

53. Without a governance structure, under who or what agencies' authority is your jurisdiction's integration efforts implemented?

❒ Centralized IT department   ❒ Individual agency   ❒ Committee

❒ Other: _____

54. Which of the following has engaged in a strategic planning process for criminal justice/public safety information systems integration?

❒ Agency/department   ❒ City   ❒ County   ❒ Regional/multijurisdictional   ❒ State   ❒ No such process

55. What were the sources of funding for the initial procurement and implementation of the integrated information system? (Check all that apply)

❒ Federal grant(s)   ❒ Private funding   ❒ Capital improvement project

❒ User fees   ❒ Not funded   ❒ Normal operating budget

❒ State funding   ❒ Not sure   ❒ Local bond issue

❒ Other: _____

56. How is the ongoing integrated system operation and maintenance funded? (Check all that apply)

❏ Federal grant(s)   ❏ Private funding   ❏ Capital improvement project
❏ User fees   ❏ Not funded   ❏ Normal operating budget
❏ State funding   ❏ Not sure   ❏ Local bond issue
❏ Other: _____   ❏ Other: _____

57. How are the enhancements/improvements to the system funded? (Check all that apply)

❏ Federal grant(s)   ❏ Private funding   ❏ Capital improvement project
❏ User fees   ❏ Not funded   ❏ Normal operating budget
❏ State funding   ❏ Not sure   ❏ Local bond issue
❏ Other: ❏ Other: _____

58. Do those criminal justice/public safety agencies involved in integration maintain separate funding accounts between existing technology and emerging technologies?   ❏ Yes   ❏ No   ❏ Varies

59. What challenges did/does your jurisdiction face in obtaining funding for integrated criminal justice/public safety technologies? Briefly explain. _____
_____

60. Does your agency use any unique/innovative mechanisms for funding integrated criminal justice / public safety information systems? If yes, briefly describe. _____
_____

All respondents please continue to section V.

Section V
Development and Barriers

All respondents please complete section V.

61. What three recommendations would you offer local jurisdictions regarding establishing local governance structures to facilitate the integration of criminal justice/public safety information systems?

1. _____
2. _____
3. _____

62. What are three major obstacles to avoid when developing and/or implementing an integrated systems governance structure?

1. _____
2. _____
3. _____

63. Please provide three recommendations you would make to criminal justice/public safety agencies with respect to the integration of information systems.

1. _____
2. _____
3. _____

64. **What are three major obstacles to avoid with respect to the integration of criminal justice/public safety information systems?**

1._____

2._____

3._____

On behalf of cities and counties nationwide, thank you for the help and advice you provided by completing this survey. It may be necessary for us to contact you for further elaboration on your responses. May we do so?

❐ Yes   ❐ No

If yes: What is the best time to call?

Name:_____

Phone:_____   E-mail:_____

Day of the Week: _____   Time: _____

Appendix B
Jurisdictions Responding to Survey

Alabama
Auburn
Huntsville
Mountain Brook
Arizona
Chandler
Mesa
Phoenix
Scottsdale
Tucson
California
Atwater
Culver City
East Palo Alto
El Cerrito
Fresno
Long Beach
Oakland
Orange
Palo Alto
Richmond
Rocklin
San Bernardino
San Diego
San Jose
Sangar
Santa Ana
Santa Cruz
Twentynine Palms
Victorville
Colorado
Castle Rock
Denver
Pueblo
Rifle
Trinadad
Wheat Ridge
Connecticut
East Hampton
Manchester
Delaware
Newark
Florida
Clearwater
Eagle Lake
Fort Lauderdale
Lake Mary
Longwood
Miami Shores
Ocala
Ponce Inlet
Sarasota
Titusville
Vero Beach
Georgia
Atlanta
Dublin

Iowa
Boone
Council Bluffs
Des Moines
Dubuque
Marion
Mason City
Spencer
Urbandale
Waterloo
Idaho
Coeur d'Alene
Paris
Illinois
Arlington Heights
Bradley
E Peoria
East Dundee
East Moline
Elk Grove Village
Fulton
Geneva
N Chicago
New Lenox
Oak Brook
Park Ridge
Romeoville
Roselle
Schaumburg
Springfield
Streamwood
Wheaton
Indiana
Greenwood
Kansas
Abilene
Chanute
Overland Park
Salina
Wichita
Kentucky
Campbellsville
Lakeside Park
Louisville
Morganfield
Louisiana
Westwego
Massachusetts
Fair Haven
Lexington
Newburyport
Maryland
Bel Air
Ellicott City
LaPlata
Salisbury

Maine
S Portland
Michigan
Alpena
Ann Arbor
Birmingham
Coldwater
Essexville
Gaylord
Grand Rapids
Grandville
Grosse Ile
Grosse Pointe Shores
Midland
Monroe
Muskegon
South Haven
Sterling Heights
Traverse City
White Cloud
Minnesota
Brooklyn Park
Fairmont
Fridley
Hastings
Mankato
Minneapolis
Perham
Pine City
Rochester
Missouri
Belton
Blue Springs
Independence
Kirkwood
Richmond Heights
Webster Groves
Montana
Missoula
North Carolina
Albemarle
Cary
Lexington
Long View
Matthews
Nags Head
Roxboro
Statesville
Warrenton
North Dakota
Beulah
Bismarck
Fargo
Nebraska
LaVista
Omaha

New Jersey
Hackensack
Moorestown
New Mexico
Santa Fe
Nevada
Reno
New York
Herkimes
Monticello
New York
Rochester
Ohio
Cincinnati
Columbus
Kettering
Springfield
Waynesville
West Carrollton
Oklahoma
Bartlesville
Coweta
Enid
Oklahoma City
Yukon
Oregon
Corvaux
Eugene
Lake Oswego
Salem
Tillamook
Tualatin
West Linn
Pennsylvania
Ardmore
Canonsburg
Carlisle
Harrisburg
Levittown
Philadelphia
Stroudsburg
Rhode Island
North Kingstown
South Carolina
Abbeville
South Dakota
Watertown
Tennessee
Fayetteville
Memphis
Red Bank

Texas
Beaumont
Brenham
Corpus Christi
Dallas
Deer Park
Fort Worth
Grand Prairie
Jacksboro
Llano
Longview
McKinney
Mt Pleasant
Plainview
Universal City
Uvalde
Victoria
Waco
Utah
Farmington
Layton
Provo
S Ogden
Virginia
Alexandria
Fairfax
Lovingston
Martinsville
Norfolk
Richmond
Rocky Mount
Stafford
Tearisburg
Vienna
Virginia Beach
Winchester
Washington
Bellevue
Camas
Seattle
Shoreline
Vancouver
Wisconsin
Hudson
Kenosha
Milwaukee
Monona
Platteville
Wausau
West Virginia
Beckley
Wyoming
Casper
Douglas

Appendix C:
Bibliography/Resources

Bibliography

Anthony Cresswell and David Connelly, Center for Technology in Government, "Reconnaissance Study: Developing a Business Case for the Integration of Criminal Justice Information," September 1999.

Cooperative Agreement for Criminal Justice Coordinating Committee Operation, Minneapolis, Minnesota and Hennepin County, Minnesota, June 1998.

Public Technology, Inc., "Local Governance Survey," March 2000

SEARCH, "Integration in the Context of Justice Information Systems: A Common Understanding," A SEARCH special report, March 2000.

U.S. Department of Justice, Office of Justice Programs, "Report of the Intergovernmental Information Sharing: Focus Group," February 24, 1998, and Conference of States, March 5 and 6, 1998.

U.S. Department of Justice, Office of Justice Programs, Office of General Counsel, "Integrated Justice Information Systems: The Department of Justice Initiative," April 2000.

U.S. Department of Justice, Office of Justice Programs, "Report of the Intergovernmental Information Sharing Conference of States," November 17 and 18, 1998.

Resources

Site Visits

Hennepin County's Criminal Justice System Information Integration Project Web site: www.macrogroup.net/cjsiip/.

Dakota County's Criminal Justice Information Integration Network Web site: www.co.dakota.mn.us/sheriff/cjiin/cjiin/htm.

San Diego County's Automated Regional Justice Information System Web site: www.arjis.org.

General

Center for Technology in Government, University at Albany, State University of New York: www.ctg.albany.edu.

National Association of State Information Resource Executives, NASIRE Justice Report—Toward National Sharing of Governmental Information: www.nasire.org.

SEARCH, The National Consortium for Justice Information and Statistics: www.search.org.

U.S. Department of Justice, Office of Justice Programs, Integrated Justice Information Technology Initiative: www.ojp.usdoj.gov/integratedjustice/.

Appendix D
Worksheets

What is your vision for the integration process? In the space below, write a statement that describes what you hope to accomplish by integrating justice information systems.

....

....

What is the mission of your integration effort? In the space below write a mission statement for your governance structure.

....

....

....

What are the goals and objectives of the integration effort? What do you want to achieve and how can you get there?

In the space below, list the goals and objectives you think are important.

....

....

....

....

What is the scope of integration?

What problems do you want to solve? ....

....

Who are the stakeholders? ....

....

Who are the lead agencies, if any? ....

....

What systems need to be integrated to solve problems you have identified? ....

....

Which and how many users would be impacted as a result of integration? ....

....

What kind of agreement do you need to create the governance board?

❏ Memorandum of Understanding   ❏ Statute or Ordinance

❏ Joint Powers Agreement   ❏ Informal Guidelines

Which agencies should be included in the governance board?

Put a checkmark by the agencies and others that should be represented on the governance board.

Law Enforcement
- ❒ Sheriff
- ❒ Police

Prosecution
- ❒ Prosecutor
- ❒ District Attorney
- ❒ County Attorney
- ❒ State's Attorney

Courts
State Supreme Court
- ❒ Judges
- ❒ Clerks
- ❒ Court Services

Courts of General Jurisdiction
- ❒ Judges
- ❒ Clerks
- ❒ Court Services

Juvenile or Family Court
- ❒ Judges
- ❒ Clerk
- ❒ Court Services

Courts of Limited or Special Jurisdiction
- ❒ Judges
- ❒ Clerk
- ❒ Court Services

Defense
- ❒ Legal Aid
- ❒ Public Defender
- ❒ Bar Association

Corrections
- ❒ Jail Administrators
- ❒ State Corrections

Probation/Parole
- ❒ County
- ❒ State
- ❒ Federal

Roles and Responsibilities of the Governance Structure.

Choose the responsibilities you want the governance structure to carry out.

Executive Responsibilities
- ❒ Provide vision and focus for the scope of the integration
- ❒ Appoint steering committees and task forces (technology, policy, management, etc.)
- ❒ Direct and coordinate the initiative
- ❒ Set policy
- ❒ Set priorities
- ❒ Review projects
- ❒ Approve projects
- ❒ Resolve conflict
- ❒ Ensure compliance
- ❒ Monitor progress
- ❒ Secure funding
- ❒ Other

Project Operations Responsibilities
- ❒ Establish policies and procedures for establishment of database and the maintenance, update, and integration of information
- ❒ Negotiate with vendor of software
- ❒ Commit staff
- ❒ Approve standards and business practices
- ❒ Keep the executive board informed
- ❒ Implementation

Planning Responsibilities
- ❒ Strategic justice information technology projects in, for example, police, court, corrections, and city attorney's office
- ❒ Determine vision, strategic plan, goals and objectives for justice information systems programs
- ❒ Implement and oversee the strategic plan
- ❒ Solicit input from all participating agencies and jurisdictions
- ❒ Determine integration needs among stakeholders

Funding and Resource Development Responsibilities
- ❒ Obtain funding
- ❒ Determine funding priorities
- ❒ Approve the annual budget
- ❒ Identify other resources
- ❒ Commit staff

Other Responsibilities

. . . .

. . . .

. . . .

What authority and powers will the governance structure have?

Executive Authority
❏ Approve strategic plan
❏ Approve annual budget
❏ Approve new projects
❏ Approve additional agencies and participating members

❏ Control funding
❏ Seek funding
❏ Approve funding
❏ Lobby for funding

Operational Authority
❏ Monitor participants for compliance to plan
❏ Evaluate against mission

To whom will the Governance Body Report?

Check all agencies or individuals to which your governance structure will report.

❏ **Participating Justice Agencies**
  ❏ Police
  ❏ Sheriff
  ❏ Prosecution
  ❏ Courts
  ❏ Defense
  ❏ Corrections
  ❏ Probation
  ❏ Parole

❏ **Elected Officials**
  ❏ City Council
  ❏ County Commission
  ❏ Mayor
  ❏ County Executive
  ❏ Chief Judge

❏ **Appointed Officials**
  ❏ City Manager
  ❏ County Manager

❏ **Funding Sources**
  ❏ Local   ❏ State
  ❏ Regional ❏ Federal

Staffing the Governance Structure. Check the appropriate item below.
Does the governance structure need a staff of its own?

❏ Yes   ❏ No   ❏ Not now, but maybe in the future

What kind of staff does the governance structure need now or in the future?

❏ Executive director❏ Budget or finance director

❏ Support staff (secretarial, etc.)   ❏ Technical staff

Where will funds to pay staff come from?

❏ Governance structure's budget   ❏ Participating agencies' contributions

❏ Participating agencies' payrolls   ❏ There won't be funds to pay staff

❏ Don't know

Commonsense Factors: Although each governance structure is unique because it reflects unique mix of goals, personalities, etc., there are several factors common to all successful ones.

Political support: Successful governance structures have a strong commitment from the chief elected and appointed officials and strong public support.

Champion or champions: In every successful governance structure is a champion—an executive, manager, an elected official— someone who saw the benefits of integration and worked to bring it about.

Participation and commitment by key stakeholders: Stakeholders shared a common goal to integrate data through an automated system, and a common need to have direction in implementing the integration efforts.

Basic technical competency: In successful efforts, the information technology people were capable of choosing, installing, and maintaining the appropriate hardware and software. The system was based on common standards for data and communications.

Sufficient resources: Successful efforts had sufficient resources (funding, personnel) dedicated to the implementation of the integration of justice information systems data.

Consistency of leadership, staff, and consultants: The successful efforts were marked by consistent leadership, stable staffs, and long-term relationships with good consultants.

Identify a core group and call a meeting: Who would you consider to be the core group of people interested in integrating justice information systems? List their names, phone numbers, and e-mail addresses below.

Information Technology
❏ Information technology directors or officers
❏ Information technology managers
❏ GIS administrators

State Agencies
❏ State Department of Motor Vehicles
❏ State Department of Boating and Waterways
❏ State Licensing Agencies
❏ State Police
❏ State Criminal Record Repository
❏ Others

Elected Officials and Government Administrators
❏ Mayor
❏ County executive
❏ City council member
❏ County commission member
❏ City manager
❏ County manager

Participants From Outside the Justice System
❏ School administration
❏ Public works/transportation
❏ Planning
❏ Fiscal planning/budget officer

❏ Health, mental health and human services
❏ Children's services
❏ Fire/emergency medical services
❏ Victim/witness organizations
❏ Environmental protection agencies
❏ Social service providers
❏ Zoning and property managers
❏ State and local department of transportation

Consultants
❏ Private Sector
❏ Other

Name	Telephone	E-Mail
. . . .		
. . . .		
. . . .		
. . . .		
. . . .		
. . . .		
. . . .		
. . . .		

NOTES

Bureau of Justice Assistance Information

General Information

Callers may contact the U.S. Department of Justice Response Center for general information or specific needs, such as assistance in submitting grant applications and information about training. To contact the Response Center, call 1–800–421–6770 or write to 1100 Vermont Avenue NW., Washington, DC 20005.

Indepth Information

For more indepth information about BJA, its programs, and its funding opportunities, requesters can call the BJA Clearinghouse. The BJA Clearinghouse, a component of the National Criminal Justice Reference Service (NCJRS), shares BJA program information with state and local agencies and community groups across the country. Information specialists are available to provide reference and referral services, publication distribution, participation and support for conferences, and other networking and outreach activities. The Clearinghouse can be reached by

❐ **Mail**
P.O. Box 6000
Rockville, MD 20849–6000

❐ **Visit**
2277 Research Boulevard
Rockville, MD 20850

❐ **Telephone**
1–800–688–4252
Monday through Friday
8:30 a.m. to 7 p.m.
eastern time

❐ **Fax**
301–519–5212

❐ **BJA Home Page**
www.ojp.usdoj.gov/BJA

❐ **NCJRS Home Page**
www.ncjrs.org

❐ **E-mail**
askncjrs@ncjrs.org

❐ **JUSTINFO Newsletter**
E-mail to listproc@ncjrs.org
Leave the subject line blank
In the body of the message,
type:
subscribe justinfo
[your name]